Edie Klein, CCD

It's My Job

Job Descriptions
for Over 30 Camp Jobs

*American Camping Association*sm

Copyright 1992 American Camping Association, Inc.
Reprint 1995

Printed in the United States of America

American Camping Association
5000 State Road 67 North
Martinsville, IN 46151-7902
317/342-8456 American Camping Association National Office
800/428-CAMP American Camping Association Bookstore
317/342-2065 FAX

Library of Congress Cataloging-in-Publications Data
Klein, Edie, 1930-
    It's my job : job descriptions for over 30 camp jobs/Edie Klein.
        p. cm.
    ISBN 0-87603-127-0
    1. Camp counselors — Job descriptions. 2. Recreation — Vocational
guidance — United States. I. Title.

GV198.C6K57 1992
796.54 — dc20   91-363924
                                                       CIP

Table of Contents

C O N T E N T S

A Note From the Author

Since I believe firmly there is more than one way to do things, I have resisted for a long time putting together the information in this book. I caution the user and reader who believes this book will give them instant job descriptions, schedules, and forms for their own camp. As you read, please pick and choose, change, add and delete information so that it meets your needs.

In most cases, the job descriptions can be used for both resident and day camps; however, I have included some notes on customizing the general counselor position for a day camp or resident camp. Just as important, you must also update job descriptions and forms to suit your needs.

I normally review job descriptions annually. It is important to rewrite descriptions based not on what *should* be done but rather on what is realistic to expect. The best people to rewrite job descriptions are those staff who have filled the positions previously.

Make job descriptions realistic. Make forms usable for your operation. Use the forms in this book as a foundation from which to build your camp's own unique forms, applications, and job descriptions.

The author thanks Camp Pine Forest, Greeley, Pennsylvania, for the opportunity to test ideas and concepts. Thanks also to Mr. David Capozzi, National Easter Seal Society, for his suggestions pertaining to meeting the intent of the Americans With Disabilities Act of 1990.

Edie Klein

An Open Letter to Camp Directors

Each year finding the right staff persons to fill the many different jobs in a camp takes a great deal of the camp director's time. A major component of that process is clearly defining essential responsibilities for each job. We hope this publication helps you to prepare the specific job descriptions necessary for your camp.

A recent federal law, the Americans With Disabilities Act, has created a great deal of confusion about employment practices. The purpose of this act is similar to all previous pieces of civil rights legislation — to eliminate as much as possible all forms of discrimination against a portion of our population.

Just as previous civil rights laws were met with resistance and confusion, this law is not being welcomed with open arms. Not many of us like to be told by the government how to do our jobs. But, when a significant portion of our population is systematically excluded from participation in many aspects of life, our government acts to eliminate factors leading to those exclusions.

We have a significant number of citizens who have been excluded from many of life's activities, not because they cannot participate in them, but because it hasn't been convenient for most of us to make the accommodations necessary for their participation.

We do not believe that the ADA will become a significant burden for camps. As you work to define the essential functions for each job description needed for your camp, we encourage you to look for ways persons with disabilities could fill the positions! We believe that persons with disabilities can become a significant asset to your camp and its programming.

This book has been developed with the ADA in mind; we think it will help you define essential functions of the jobs included. Each camp must make modifications to account for the unique characteristics of its operation. As you do that, consider the unique perspective that persons with disabilities could add to your staff.

John A. Miller

Executive Vice President
American Camping Association, Inc.

Creating Your Own Job Descriptions

Before you jump headfirst into writing or updating your program's job descriptions, please carefully read this introduction.

Job descriptions are important tools for any business or operation, and camp is no exception. When carefully and professionally crafted, job descriptions serve to inform job applicants, guide employees, and can serve as a reference to assess an employee's performance.

Why Job Descriptions Are Important

For the Employer

The success of your program depends on how well your staff performs. Well-written job descriptions are essential to building your staff. They help you hire the most qualified people, define staff training needs (e.g., which abilities do you expect staff members to have and which do you expect to teach them), and appraise staff performance.

For the Employee

Job descriptions are crucial for an employee's understanding of the abilities and job skills he or she must possess, his or her relationship to other employees, and the duties that are required and will be the basis of performance reviews.

Determining Who's Qualified

The Americans With Disabilities Act, passed in 1990, provides all of us with a new awareness of and responsibility to persons of all abilities. The ADA states it is unlawful to discriminate against a qualified individual who has a disability *because* of that disability. The term "qualified individual with a disability" refers to a person with a disability who, with or without reasonable accommodations, can perform the essential functions of the job. All employers must therefore identify the *essential* functions, as opposed to the *marginal* functions, of each job.

How to Create a Job Description

All elements of a job description should relate directly to the particular setting in which the job will be accomplished. Whether you are starting from scratch or are choosing a job description from this book or another source as a model, it is important that you understand all the elements of a job description so you can customize the information to best represent the job in your program.

As you adapt these models to your own program's needs, consider these kinds of issues: which jobs your program has; how combinations of responsibilities listed here fit together in one position in your camp; camp goals and philosophies; camp procedures and policies; staff-training methods and time frames; the physical setting of the program; and equipment-maintenance requirements.

There are specific elements that must be included in any job description to make it an effective tool for the employer and the employee, and for compliance with ADA. The order in which these elements appear on the job description is not important. Their order should be dictated only by what seems logical to you. Additionally, what you call these elements or sections of the job descriptions is not as important as simply including all the elements.

Within each job description in this book you will find examples of the desired qualifications, line of responsibility, and general responsibilities of the job. These should be considered examples only; you will need to alter these examples to fit your program. In addition, these job descriptions will encourage you to identify the essential functions of the job.

To best serve your needs and your employees' needs, your job descriptions should include all of the following elements. These elements are described in more detail later in this chapter.

- **Position:** This is commonly a two-or-more-word descriptor of the job.
- **Desired Qualifications:** Certifications, training, and education necessary for the job are addressed here.
- **Responsible To:** This is the supervisor, or whom the person doing the job is directly responsible to.
- **General and Specific Responsibilities:** These are descriptions of task-related responsibilities of the job. They are generally statements describing what happens in the job.

- **Essential Functions:** These are statements of performance or ability necessary to fulfill the essential functions of the job. They are "how" and "how much" statements describing what it takes to do the job. Qualitative and quantitative terms should be used. To assist in compliance with the Americans With Disabilities Act of 1990, auditory, visual, ambulatory, mobility, cognitive, and communication abilities should be considered here.

Desired Qualifications

Qualifications are those skills, certifications, training, or other experiences pre-requisite to holding the job. One assumes the applicant comes to the position with those prerequisites having been met. Consult the American Camping Association camp accreditation standards for some of the recommended qualifications.

When identifying the qualifications for each job, list only those truly necessary for the position. They should be reasonable and justifiable. Qualification statements should be carefully crafted to avoid discrimination; in other words, be sure the skills listed don't automatically exclude persons with disabilities.

For instance, if you cannot defend that the job includes or might include driving responsibilities, do not include holding a driver's license as a qualification. It might be considered discriminatory if driving is not an essential function of the job. If you require some proof of identification for employment, you might broaden this statement to include other kinds of picture identification which also gives appropriate information.

Age should not be listed as a qualification unless there is a specific reason a person of a particular age would be essential to the job. For example, it would not be appropriate to list an age qualification such as *between the ages of 18 and 30* for camp positions simply because you want young people to apply. Federal and state laws prohibit discrimination of persons over 40, and therefore a maximum age requirement should not be listed.

On the other hand, it may be appropriate to use a minimum age requirement for positions that demand a higher maturity level. It is quite acceptable to request that applicants for counselor positions *be 18 years old or have completed at least one year of college.*

In your search for food service staff, you may need someone who is able to carry 50-pound bags of food across the kitchen. The ADA regulations suggest a job description be specific in naming how much, how high, how often, and how many. Therefore, qualifications for these positions may say, for example *ability to lift objects weighing up to 50 pounds, carry them several feet, and place them on a three-foot-high counter, a minimum of three times a day (at each meal preparation)*.

A phrase like *able-bodied worker* does not describe the necessary qualifications. This statement would not assist you in selecting the right candidate, and would not provide the employee with the necessary expectations of the job. It could also bring a charge of discrimination.

General and Specific Responsibilities

This section identifies duties that will be carried out on the job. These responsibilities, duties, or tasks, may require skills already attained by the applicant, or they may require training by the camp's administrative or program staff, generally during pre-camp training. Prerequisite skills should be addressed under "desired qualifications."

There are at least a couple of ways to set up this section of your job descriptions. One way would be to list each specific responsibility under one general statement of responsibility. Another way would be to create three or four categories of responsibilities with a general responsibility as the beginning of each category.

This book presents examples primarily of one general statement of responsibility, followed by a list of specific responsibilities. Listing each specific responsibility separately, without categorizing them, gives attention to the specific tasks of a job. For example:

- **Position:** Adventure/Ropes Course Program Director
- **General Responsibilities:** To plan, direct, and supervise the camp's adventure/ropes course program.
- **Specific Responsibilities:**
  1. Set up adventure/ropes course prior to and during staff training.
  2. Teach staff responsibilities in activity area during staff training.
  3. Teach and monitor proper use of equipment.
  4. Conduct initial and end-of-season inventory, and store equipment.
  5. Check equipment and make (or file for) necessary repairs.
  6. Check lesson plans for all activities.
  7. Keep records on all participants; help them progress from beginner to advanced levels.

8. Follow standard rules applicable to ropes course, rappelling, etc.
9. Submit orders for equipment and/or supplies when needed, ensuring timely arrival of materials.
10. Evaluate current season and make recommendations for equipment, supplies, and program for following season.

Another way to set up this section is to break the jobs into three or four general responsibilities, rather than just one, and group those specific responsibilities under these. Categorizing responsibilities may give the staff member a different view of the various types of duties. The head counselor and general counselor job descriptions in this book are set up this way. Additionally, the previous ropes course director's general responsibility could be split into the following *four* general responsibilities.

- **Position:** Adventure/Ropes Course Program Director
- **General Responsibility:** Train campers and staff in the activity.
- **Specific Responsibilities:**
  1. Teach staff their responsibilities in activity during pre-camp training.
  2. Check lesson plans for all activities.
  3. Coordinate in-service training for ropes course staff.
  4. Teach proper use of equipment.
- **General Responsibility:** Supervise campers, staff, and program.
- **Specific Responsibilities:**
  1. Keep records on all participants; help them progress from beginner to advanced levels.
  2. Follow standard rules applicable to ropes course, rappelling, etc.
- **General Responsibility:** Monitor the facilities and equipment of the activity.
- **Specific Responsibilities:**
  1. Set up adventure/ropes course prior to and during staff training.
  2. Conduct initial, daily, and end-of-season check of equipment for safety, cleanliness, and good repair. Store equipment for safety.
  3. Make or file for necessary repairs.
  4. Submit orders for equipment and/or supplies when needed, ensuring timely arrival of materials.

5. Monitor proper use of equipment.
6. Assist in packing equipment for following season.
- **General Responsibility:** Evaluate program, staff, and facilities of the activity and make recommendations.
- **Specific Responsibilities:**
    1. Maintain appropriate stock of materials for program.
    2. Evaluate current season and make recommendations for equipment, supplies, and program for following season.

Addressing Your Camp's Goals

A staff member's responsibility to carry out the goals of the camp or program should be reflected in each job description, typically in the general and specific responsibilities section. If you decide to list all specifics under one general statement of responsibility, you might include in that list statements that addresses how the employee serves to carry out the program goals. In an activity counselor's job description, the following are examples of reflections of the camp's goals.

- **Position:** Activity Counselor
- **General Responsibility:** To assist in teaching a skill or activity and maintaining standards that lead to a quality program.
- **Specific Responsibilities:**
    1. Encourage individuality and creativity in participants.
    2. Help participants develop a sense of fair play, to accept both winning and losing graciously.
    3. Help cabin group function cooperatively as a unit.
    4. Encourage understanding and sensitivity to the natural environment.
    5. Encourage respect for individuals and their differences.

If you opt to split one general responsibility into three or four general responsibilities, you might use a general-responsibility statement like the following to address program goals. For example:

- **Position:** Athletic Counselor
- **General Responsibility:** Plan and supervise participant activities that contribute to program goals and individual development.
- **Specific Responsibilities:**
    1. Help participants develop a sense of fair play, to accept both winning and losing graciously.

2. Plan and conduct activities that allow participants of all ability levels to enjoy themselves and experience success.
3. Etc.

Essential Functions

The Americans With Disabilities Act mandates that it is unlawful to discriminate against persons who are able to fulfill the *essential functions* of the job, with or without reasonable accommodation. It is helpful, therefore, for the director to identify those functions or duties in the job description.

When developing general and specific responsibilities, you listed tasks a staff member fulfills. Now in this section you should step back from specific tasks and identify the overall essential functions of the job — what must the staff member do to accomplish those tasks. Note this term is "essential functions," not "marginal functions."

Essential functions are critical responsibilities to fulfilling the intent of the job. A marginal function is one often carried out by a person in that position, but is not absolutely essential. For instance, it is *essential* that staff be able to communicate effectively to enforce safety regulations. On the other hand, helping campers make up their bunks is a *marginal* function of the counselor's role. Someone other than the cabin counselor could do that part of the job. If all counselors cannot do this, the safety of the campers will not be jeopardized.

There is no universal or definitive method to determine whether a responsibility is an essential function. However, you *might* judge a responsibility to be an essential function if the position exists to perform this responsibility; if, due to the number of employees, the task cannot be distributed (shared or moved to another job description); if there is a certain degree of skill or specialization required to perform the function; or if an inability to perform the function creates a risk to the employee, the organization, or the participants.

In writing essential-functions statements, you must also identify the abilities required to fulfill the function. It is important to focus on the abilities necessary for the job rather than disabilities that might disqualify an applicant. Ask yourself which of the following abilities are required to fulfill the responsibilities you have identified as essential.

- **Auditory ability**
- **Visual ability**
- **Ambulatory ability**

- **Cognitive ability**
- **Communication ability**
- **Physical ability or strength**

For each ability listed, ask yourself what level of performance is required by the person in this job. For instance, while the camp secretary needs to get from place to place in the central camp area, it should not be assumed that walking is required. The essential function is the ability to complete errands throughout the central part of camp. It would be inappropriate to identify walking as an essential function since that defines an ability not necessary to complete the task in this instance.

Not all jobs will require all the abilities listed here. Like every other element of a job description, the essential functions will be defined by the setting, activities, and goals of your specific program. For instance, a general counselor's position may identify the following.

- **Position:** General Counselor
- **Essential Functions:**
  1. Ability to communicate and work with groups participating (age and skill levels), and provide necessary instruction to campers.
  2. Abilities to observe camper behavior, assess its appropriateness, enforce appropriate safety regulations and emergency procedures, and apply appropriate behavior-management techniques.
  3. Visual and auditory ability to identify and respond to environmental and other hazards related to the activity.

The following is an example of what the essential functions of the job might be for an adventure/ropes course director position.

- **Position:** Adventure/Ropes Course Program Director
- **Essential Functions:**
  1. Ability to communicate and train staff and campers in safety regulations and emergency procedures.
  2. Visual and auditory ability to identify and respond to environmental and other hazards related to the activity.
  3. Ability to communicate and work with groups participating (age and skill levels), and provide necessary instruction to campers and/or staff.
  4. Physical strength to spot and belay participants.
  5. Abilities to observe camper behavior, assess its appropriateness, enforce appropriate safety

regulations and emergency procedures, and apply appropriate behavior-management techniques.

6. Physical ability to respond appropriately to situations requiring first aid.

7. Cognitive and communication abilities to plan and conduct the activity to achieve camper development objectives.

The following are examples of particular considerations in specific jobs you will want to keep in mind when you address their essential functions. (Note: You should have addressed related certifications, trainings, or other experience in the "desired qualifications" section.)

- **Business manager** — must be able to use computer; use phone; order supplies; drive to pick up supplies; carry and load supplies; keep neat and orderly records.

- **Secretary** — must be able to use office equipment; use telephone; relate to camper needs; handle and file records; and complete errands to town (driving?) and throughout camp.

- **Maintenance supervisor** — **must be able to use equipment and tools; drive around camp property; observe what needs to be done; communicate with staff; have physical strength (to lift, dig, load, unload, mop, repair, etc.).**

- **Nurse** — must be able to drive to doctor or emergency treatment locations; lift/assist campers or staff; read prescriptions and health exams from physicians; get to remote locations on camp property quickly; use telephone; observe and assess unsanitary or unhealthy conditions of camp.

- **Food service personnel** — **must be able to lift/unload/ move food and supplies; lift dishes to their storage location; use kitchen equipment safely; operate electrical and mechanical equipment; maintain appropriate inventory of food and supplies; operate dishwasher while maintaining appropriate temperature; determine cleanliness of dishes, food contact surfaces, and kitchen area; assess condition of food.**

- **Program directors** — must be able to train staff; observe camper behavior; identify and respond to hazards; work with different age and skill levels; and plan and conduct activity.

- **Counseling staff** — must be able to assist campers in emergency (fire, evacuation, illness, or injury); drive (especially for day camps); observe loading and unloading of buses and vans (especially in day camps); and possess strength and endurance required to maintain constant supervision of campers.

According to ADA, even if an essential function can not met by an otherwise qualified applicant, if that function can be met with or without reasonable accommodations, the job should be given to the most qualified applicant regardless of disability. For example: if an applicant for the adventure/ropes course program director position has all of the qualifications for the position except *physical strength to spot and belay participants,* it would be considered a reasonable accommodation to have an additional staff member on site to spot and belay. This applicant, therefore still qualifies for the job.

Reasonable accommodation, as defined in ADA, refers to an accommodation that can be made without undo hardship to the employer. *Undo hardship,* as defined by the Equal Employment Opportunity Commission, is an action requiring significant difficulty or expense (i.e., an action that is unduly costly, extensive, substantial, or disruptive, or that fundamentally alters the nature of the business). You must consider all reasonable accommodations to allow an individual to do a job. Some costly accommodations may be deemed reasonable by the EEOC.

The essential functions of the job should truly be essential; they must be reasonable and justifiable. Is it necessary for a secretary to have the ability to type 90 words per minute? Is it necessary for a staff member to have verbal ability, or might another form of communication be acceptable? Job descriptions written in a discriminatory manner will not shield the employer from liability.

Properly written job descriptions are not the end-all or the purpose of ADA. They would, therefore, not be the sole evidence used in determining compliance with the law. There are other aspects of your operation that require review for compliance. They include staff-hiring procedures; staff-training methods; supervision of employees; employer judgement in hiring; experience levels of persons in similar jobs; rationale for qualifications and essential functions; and requirements of similar jobs.

All of this may sound a little overwhelming. The best way to make your camp comply with ADA is to start with something achievable in one year, such as rewriting your job descriptions.

No one can force you to hire someone who is unqualified for the job (i.e., someone who lacks the minimum qualifications or someone who cannot perform the essential functions of the job even with reasonable accommodation). The intent of the Americans With Disabilities Act is to allow qualified individuals who have a disability to more easily become an active part of our workforce.

How This Book Is Organized

Finding the Job Descriptions You Want

The job descriptions in this book are divided into three broad categories: operational jobs, program jobs, and the director position. You will find food service, maintenance, office, and health care positions in the operations section. The program director, program assistant, and counseling positions are located in the program section. The camp director position is listed in a section by itself.

All jobs covered in this book are listed in the table of contents and in an alphabetical cross-reference index in the back of the book.

What the Job Descriptions Include

Within each job description in this book you will find examples of desired qualifications, line of responsibility, and general and specific responsibilities of the job. These should be considered examples only. You should tailor these examples to fit *your* program.

Each job description also includes specific reminders to adapt the information to your program — to address your own program's goals and to address the essential functions of the job as it occurs in your program. Information on how to do this is covered earlier in this chapter.

More

Information about interviewing staff, staff training, and counselor-in-training programs begins on page 79.

For more information on the Americans With Disabilities Act and how it could affect your camp operations, contact the American Camping Association, 5000 State Road 67 North, Martinsville, Ind., 46151-7902; or contact the U.S. Department of Justice, Civil Rights Division, P.O. Box 66118, Washington, D.C. 20035-6118.

Definitions of Terms

- **Activity, department, or program heads** — persons in complete charge of a program and the staff related to that program (i.e., aquatics head who directs different programs and staff in the area of swimming, boating, canoeing and sailing).
- **Counselor** — direct relationship with staff, lives with campers or has direct responsibility for a group.
- **Staff training** — time set aside for in-camp staff training prior to the arrival of the campers. This time is sometimes referred to as counselor camp.
- **Health center** — terms used interchangeably, to denote a building or area set aside for prevention of health problems and for health care. The health center is sometimes referred to as the infirmary.
- **Key staff** — unit leader, head counselor or higher position; for example, activity or department heads.
- **Staff member** — any position at camp.
- **Unit or division** — area within camp divided into smaller groups with a key staff member as the supervisor. Usually age- or program-restricted; grouping of programs. Could be a designation for program purposes only.
- **Unit leader/head counselor** — supervisor of a camp unit or a camp division.

Camp Director

Desired Qualifications

- Bachelors in camp administration or related degree. Director certification by the American Camping Association preferred
- Current CPR and first aid certifications
- At least one season of camp administrative experience (i.e., unit leader, head counselor)
- Ability to supervise staff and campers
- Ability to meet the public
- Ability to plan, originate, organize, and carry out daily and special programs

Responsible To

Camp owner, agency's camp coordinator, or board of directors

 ## Camp Goals

This job description should include specific responsibilities to help identify and define the goals of the camp and the goals of camper development, and/or reflect the director's role in carrying out these goals as defined by organization. For examples, see pages 8-9.

General Responsibility

To plan, direct, and supervise all camp programs and staff.

Specific Responsibilities

1. Define camp goals and/or define and plan program to reflect camp goals.
2. Originate and carry out a system for recruiting campers and staff utilizing brochures, telephone calls, reunions, hot prospect lists, etc.
3. Prepare and conduct pre-camp and in-service staff trainings.
4. Order or supervise the ordering of food, supplies, and equipment, and arrange for proper distribution.

5. Set and supervise office procedures, opening- and closing-day procedures for staff and campers.
6. Develop routines, schedules, and procedures for camp operation.
7. Assign staff activities and other responsibilities.
8. Assign staff and campers to cabins or groups.
9. Supervise and evaluate, or supervise evaluations of, all operations and program staff.
10. Maintain and review records and evaluations of all programs, operations, staff, and facilities.
11. Prepare an evaluation and summary of current season including inventories, staff evaluations, camper reports, and recommendations for the following season.
12. Define and monitor crisis management plan, including emergency procedures.
13. Organize and/or approve trips out of camp for program, supplies, and crisis management.
14. Monitor safety and all procedures as they pertain to the complete supervision of all campers and staff.
15. Help provide an atmosphere for developing good morale and well-being among the camp family.
16. These are not the only duties to be performed. Some duties may be reassigned and other duties may be assigned as required.

 ## Essential Functions

This job description should also identify the essential functions of the job, including any physical, cognitive, visual, auditory, and other abilities essential to fulfilling the job. See pages 9-13 for an explanation of how to determine "essential functions," and for examples of those functions. Also see page 11 for examples of particular considerations for specific jobs to keep in mind when identifying essential functions.

Business Manager

Desired Qualifications

- Ability to manage business concerns of camp
- Experience and/or education in general accounting procedures
- Experience with payroll accounting
- Ability and desire to work in a camp setting
- Good character, integrity, adaptability, and enthusiasm
- At least one season of camp administrative experience (i.e., unit leader, head counselor)
- Current CPR and first aid certifications preferred

Responsible To

Camp director

 ### Camp Goals

This job description should include specific responsibilities that reflect the position's role in carrying out the goals of the camp and the goals of camper development. For examples, see pages 8-9.

General Responsibility

To manage the camp's business concerns.

Specific Responsibilities

1. Pay or supervise payment of all camp bills as approved by camp director or appropriate personnel.
2. Process payroll and file tax reports as required.
3. Receive and/or account for all accounts receivable.
4. Set up and maintain petty cash system.
5. Prepare meaningful financial statements for camp director or camp board.
6. Handle all financial accounting on registration day(s), including receipts, bank deposits, and other financial records.
7. Supervise sales and inventory of camp trading post.

8. Process orders for camp supplies.
9. Purchase supplies as needed from local merchants.
10. Prepare bank reconciliations.
11. These are not the only duties to be performed. Some duties may be reassigned and other duties may be assigned as required.

 Essential Functions

This job description also needs to identify the essential functions of the job, including the any physical, cognitive, visual, auditory, and other abilities essential to fulfilling the job. See pages 9-13 for an explanation of how to determine "essential functions," and for examples of those functions. Also see page 11 for examples of particular considerations for specific jobs to keep in mind when identifying essential functions.

Secretary

Desired Qualifications

- Experience in office procedures (i.e., filing, answering telephones, photocopying, meeting public, etc.)
- Ability to use a word processor (computer or typewriter)
- Ability to accept guidance and supervision
- Good character, integrity, and adaptability
- Enthusiasm, sense of humor, patience, and self-control
- Desire and ability to work in a camp setting
- Current CPR and first aid certifications preferred
- 1 year of college or 18 years of age

Responsible To

Camp director and/or assistant camp director

Camp Goals

This job description should include specific responsibilities that reflect the position's role in carrying out the goals of the camp and the goals of camper development. For examples, see pages 8-9.

General Responsibility

To facilitate the work of the camp's director, assistant director, and business manager.

Specific Responsibilities

1. Assist the camp director in setting up camp office.
2. Store and keep equipment in good condition.
3. Answer phones and take accurate messages.
4. Keep office and surrounding area clean and neat.
5. Sort or oversee the sorting of camp mail and prepare outgoing mail.
6. Coordinate work coming into and out of the office (i.e., photocopying, word processing, producing program materials, etc.).

7. Explain camp office policies and procedures to all staff during staff training.
8. Be courteous and help expedite office business and the handling of any office concerns.
9. Be familiar and follow through with camp policies regarding camper and staff phone calls and messages.
10. Conduct initial and end-of-season inventory of all office equipment and supplies.
11. Order supplies as needed, ensuring timely arrival of materials.
12. Pack all office materials and supplies when season ends.
13. Evaluate current season and make recommendations for office equipment, supplies, and procedures for following season.
14. These are not the only duties to be performed. Some duties may be reassigned and other duties may be assigned as required.

▶ Essential Functions

This job description also needs to identify the essential functions of the job, including any physical, cognitive visual, auditory, and other abilities essential to fulfilling the job. See pages 9-13 for an explanation of how to determine "essential functions," and for examples of those functions. Also see page 11 for examples of particular considerations for specific jobs to keep in mind when identifying essential functions.

Food Service Manager

Desired Qualifications

- Experience in a camp or institutional food-service setting
- Supervisory skills
- Ability to relate well to others
- Registered dietician preferred
- Desire and ability to work in a camp setting

Responsible To

Camp director

 ## Camp Goals

This job description should include specific responsibilities that reflect the position's role in carrying out the goals of the camp and the goals of camper development. For examples, see pages 8-9.

General Responsibility

To plan, direct, and supervise camp's food service.

Specific Responsibilities

1. Supervise and coordinate activities of chefs, cooks, and food-service personnel.
2. Supervise dish-washing program.
3. Plan menus and utilize leftovers.
4. Hire and train staff.
5. Maintain time and payroll records.
6. Supervise pantry and storeroom.
7. Supervise preparation of food.
8. Supervise food-service-employee housing areas.
9. Approve orders, and help receive and store food and other supplies.
10. Meet with other administrative staff as necessary.
11. These are not the only duties to be performed. Some duties may be reassigned and other duties may be assigned as required.

Essential Functions

This job description should also identify the essential functions of the job, including any physical, cognitive, visual, auditory, and other abilities that are essential to fulfilling the job. See pages 9-13 for an explanation of how to determine "essential functions," and for examples of those functions. Also see page 11 for examples of particular considerations for specific jobs to keep in mind when identifying essential functions.

Head Chef

Desired Qualifications

- Experience as cook and/or assistant chef, preferably at a camp
- Training and experience in cooking for large groups
- Ability to work well with others at camp
- Ability to prepare foods for special groups (i.e., people with eating disorders, diabetes, etc.) as needed
- Knowledge of standards of food preparation, serving, and kitchen procedures

Responsible To

Food service manager

 ## Camp Goals

This job description should include specific responsibilities that reflect the position's role in carrying out goals of the camp and goals of camper development. For examples, see pages 8-9.

General Responsibilities

1. Train kitchen staff.
2. Participate in overall camp staff training.
3. Estimate needs, order, receive, and store foodstuffs and supplies.
4. Cook, trim, portion, carve, bake, etc. Portion meats, vegetables, salads, breads, deserts, etc.
5. Supervise kitchen staff, cooking, cleanliness, and scheduling of personnel.
6. Coordinate and participate with the cook and other kitchen personnel engaged in food preparation.
7. Record quantities, types, and preparation methods of food served.
8. Arrange with other kitchen supervisors for snacks, special events, and cleanliness.
9. Evaluate current season and make suggestions for following season.

10. These are not the only duties to be performed. Some duties may be reassigned and other duties may be assigned as required.

 ## Essential Functions

This job description also needs to identify the essential functions of the job, including any physical, cognitive, visual, auditory, and other abilities essential to fulfilling the job. See pages 9-13 for an explanation of how to determine the "essential functions," and for examples of those functions. Also see page 11 for examples of particular considerations for specific jobs to keep in mind when identifying essential functions.

Cook

Desired Qualifications

- Experience as cook and/or assistant cook, preferably at a camp
- Training and experience in cooking for large groups
- Ability to work well with others at camp
- Ability to prepare foods for special groups (i.e., people with eating disorders, diabetes, etc.) as needed
- Knowledge of standards of food preparation and serving, and kitchen procedures

Responsible To

Head chef

Camp Goals

This job description should include specific responsibilities that reflect the position's role in carrying out the goals of the camp and the goals of camper development. For examples, see pages 8-9.

General Responsibilities

1. Train kitchen staff with chef.
2. Participate in overall camp staff training.
3. Work with head chef to estimate needs, and to order, receive, and store foodstuffs and supplies.
4. Fry, boil, broil, roast, steam meat, poultry and/or vegetables.
5. Prepare soups and gravies.
6. Short-order cook, bake or butcher as needed.
7. Function as general all-round cook for all meals and special events.
8. In seasonal operation, clean and prepare food service areas for use. Close kitchen down for off-season.
9. Evaluate current season and make recommendations for following season.

10. These are not the only duties to be performed. Some duties may be reassigned and other duties may be assigned as required.

 Essential Functions

This job description also needs to identify the essential functions of the job, including any physical, cognitive, visual, auditory, and other abilities that are essential to fulfilling the job. See pages 9-13 for an explanation of how to determine "essential functions," and for examples of those functions. Also see page 11 for examples of particular considerations for specific jobs to keep in mind when identifying essential functions.

Food Service Assistant or Cook's Helper

Desired Qualifications

- Desire to work in the food service area
- Ability to read menus, weights, and measures
- Ability to work well with others
- Ability to accept supervision

Responsible To

Head chef

 ## Camp Goals

This job description should include specific responsibilities that reflect the position's role in carrying out the goals of the camp and the goals of camper development. For examples, see pages 8-9.

General Responsibilities

1. Assist workers in preparing foods by performing any combination of the following tasks:
    a. wash, peel, etc., vegetables;
    b. prepare poultry and meats;
    c. prepare breads;
    d. stir and strain soups and vegetables;
    e. weigh and measure foods;
    f. carry pans, pots, etc.;
    g. store food;
    h. clean utensils and area; and
    i. distribute food and supplies.
2. Assist in any area of kitchen or dining room, as requested by head cook.
3. Food service assistants may be asked to share responsibilities of the following jobs. These jobs could be designated by the cook and food service manager's assistant as:

  a. cook's helper;

  b. pot washer;

  c. pantry and salad person;

  d. dishwasher.

4. Help unload and store supplies.

5. Help move supplies around kitchen.

6. These are not the only duties to be performed. Some duties may be reassigned and other duties may be assigned as required.

 ## Essential Functions

This job description also needs to identify the essential functions of the job, including any physical, cognitive, visual, auditory, and other abilities that are essential to fulfilling the job. See pages 9-13 for an explanation of how to determine "essential functions," and for examples of those functions. Also see page 11 for examples of particular considerations for specific jobs to keep in mind when identifying essential functions.

Kitchen Helper/Dishwasher

Desired Qualifications

- Desire to work in a camp kitchen
- Ability to learn to do tasks as assigned
- Ability to accept supervision
- Ability to work well with others

Responsible To

Food service manager

Camp Goals

This job description should include specific responsibilities that reflect the position's role in carrying out the goals of the camp and the goals of camper development. For examples, see pages 8-9.

General Responsibilities

1. Wash dishes, glasses and silverware by hand or machine.
2. Sweep and mop kitchen and dining room.
3. Take out trash from kitchen and dining room to dumpster.
4. Clean and wash trash cans at least every other day, daily if needed.
5. Cut, peel, and wash vegetables, as needed.
6. Wash pots and pans, as needed.
7. Mix juice, and serve juice, milk, and water.
8. Help unload supply truck and put supplies away.
9. Clean spillage in kitchen or dining room.
10. Make sure dishwasher area is kept clean. Straighten counter and clean after each meal.
11. Help in any area of kitchen or dining room as requested by food service manager.
12. These are not the only duties to be performed. Some duties may be reassigned and other duties may be assigned as required.

Essential Functions

This job description also needs to identify the essential functions of the job, including any physical, cognitive, visual, auditory, and other abilities that are essential to fulfilling the job. See pages 9-13 for an explanation of how to determine "essential functions," and for examples of those functions. Also see page 11 for examples of particular considerations for specific jobs to keep in mind when identifying essential functions.

Dining Room Supervisor

Desired Qualifications

- Experience in a camp setting or an institutional food-service setting
- Ability to supervise campers and staff
- Ability to work well with others
- Desire and ability to work in a camp setting

Responsible to

Food service manager

 ## Camp Goals

This job description should include specific responsibilities that reflect the position's role in carrying out the goals of the camp and the goals of camper development. For examples, see pages 8-9.

General Responsibilities

1. Participate in pre-camp training for all staff.
2. Train staff and campers in management of food service as it pertains to them (i.e., time to set tables for each meal).
3. Put out sample setting of utensils for each meal, set utensils out for table-setters.
4. Inspect dining room for cleanliness and readiness for each meal.
5. Plan appropriate utensils and methods for serving each meal.
6. Contact the camp director immediately if a meal is to be late or if there are other problems.
7. Supervise camper-waiters' responsibility of:
   a. cleaning and setting tables;
   b. bringing food to the tables;
   c. putting perishables on the table;
   d. clearing and cleaning tables, trays, totes; and
   e. sweeping the floor after each meal.

8. Clean dining-hall bathroom facilities before each meal. Stock, as necessary, with paper towels, toilet paper, and soap.
9. Have floor spills cleaned up immediately.
10. Act as liaison for special food needs and orders for parties, overnight camping, day trips, special events, counselor snacks, vegetarian meals, diabetic meals, etc.
11. Arrange coverage for days off.
12. Check outside dining hall and kitchen grounds for cleanliness.
13. Provide brooms, cleaner, and cloths to wipe tables.
14. Inspect dining hall and supervise during meals. Report unnecessary roughhousing, noise, waste, or poor manners to camp director.
15. Work with health center staff on food supply and requests needed.
16. These are not the only duties to be performed. Some duties may be reassigned and other duties may be assigned as required.

▶ **Essential Functions**

This job description also needs to identify the essential functions of the job, including any physical, cognitive, visual, auditory, and other abilities that are essential to fulfilling the job. See pages 9-13 for an explanation of how to determine "essential functions," and for examples of those functions. Also see page 11 for examples of particular considerations for specific jobs to keep in mind when identifying essential functions.

Pot Washer/Cook's Helper

Desired Qualifications

- Desire and ability to work in a camp setting
- Ability to relate well with others
- Ability to accept supervision

Responsible To

Food service manager

 ## Camp Goals

This job description should include specific responsibilities that reflect the position's role in carrying out the goals of the camp and the goals of camper development. For examples, see pages 8-9.

General Responsibilities

1. Wash pots by hand or machine, as needed.
2. May peel, cut, wash vegetables.
3. Clean ovens and stoves.
4. Keep pot-washing area and floors clean.
5. Help in any area of kitchen or dining room as requested by food service manager, cook, or assistant.
6. These are not the only duties to be performed. Some duties may be reassigned and other duties may be assigned as required.

 ## Essential Functions

This job description also needs to identify the essential functions of the job, including any physical, cognitive, visual, auditory, and other abilities that are essential to fulfilling the job. See pages 9-13 for an explanation of how to determine "essential functions," and for examples of those functions. Also see page 11 for examples of particular considerations for specific jobs to keep in mind when identifying essential functions.

Maintenance Supervisor

Desired Qualifications

- Mature, capable, mechanically-oriented person
- Skill in various building trades preferable (i.e., electrical, plumbing, painting, construction, etc.)
- Ability to accept guidance and supervision from, and work with others
- Desire to live and work in a camp community
- Self-starter and organizer
- Current CPR and first aid certifications preferred

Responsible To

Camp director or organization's camp committee

 ## Camp Goals

This job description should include specific responsibilities that reflect the position's role in carrying out the goals of the camp and the goals of camper development. For examples, see pages 8-9.

General Responsibility

To maintain the grounds and facilities of camp.

Specific Responsibilities

1. Supervise and coordinate maintenance activities and assistants engaged in maintenance activities on a contract basis.
2. Maintain facilities for trash collection company, gas company, and electric company, etc.
3. Attend staff training as time permits.
4. Assist in moving materials and supplies to appropriate areas in camp as needed.
5. Maintain inventory of maintenance supplies and equipment.

6. Order equipment and supplies as needed, within budget or with approval of camp director, ensuring timely arrival of materials.
7. Be available or have maintenance staff available during all times when campers are present for emergencies.
8. Be acquainted with community fire, police, and emergency service departments.
9. Prepare any facility needing outside contract work for easy accessibility by contractors.
10. Keep and maintain fleet of vehicles in good operating condition. Repair, or supervise repair by outside service company.
11. Maintain grounds to reduce risk of danger or injury to persons using grounds and facilities.
12. Maintain wells and pumps in good operating condition to meet water standards. Maintain grounds around wells and pumps.
13. Monitor sewer system.
14. Be knowledgeable of applicable state and federal regulations pertaining to sewer, water, garbage, electrical, and water standards.
15. Maintain grounds in off-season as recommended in consultation with camp director. Arrange jobs to take advantage of differing weather conditions. Annual jobs may include:
    a. Check and repair chairs and benches;
    b. Prepare all vehicles for in-season use;
    c. Repair and/or rebuild docks;
    d. Inspect and make necessary repairs on all doors, screen doors, windows, floor boards, rafters, plumbing, porches, roofs, etc.;
    e. Inspect all buildings and paint when necessary;
    f. Inspect and repair dining room tables and picnic tables;
    g. Inspect camp for trees that may need thinning, limbs removed, etc. Prepare trees or supervise contracted tree maintenance work;
    h. Repair and adjust all small motors (i.e., mowers, blowers, cutters, etc.);
    i. Maintain inventory of beds and mattresses;
    j. Repair items recommended by staff (i.e., boats, canoes, kilns, etc.).
16. Communicate daily with camp director when possible, and set up a workable and productive schedule.

17. Complete reports, bi-annually, for review by camp director on progress, problems, and projections for repairs and replacement.
18. These are not the only duties to be performed. Some duties may be reassigned and other duties may be assigned as required.

 ## Essential Functions

This job description also needs to identify the essential functions of the job, including any physical, cognitive, visual, auditory, mobility, ambulatory, and other abilities essential to fulfilling the job. See pages 9-13 for an explanation of how to determine "essential functions," and for examples of those functions. Also see page 11 for examples of particular considerations for specific jobs to keep in mind when identifying essential functions.

Driver

Desired Qualifications

- Valid and appropriate state driver's license
- Good driving record (should be checked by insurance company)
- Current first aid and CPR certifications
- Ability to teach others proper behavior in a vehicle
- Desire and ability to work with children
- Ability to relate to one's peer group
- Ability to accept guidance, supervision, instruction
- Good character, integrity, and adaptability
- Enthusiasm, sense of humor, patience, and self-control

Responsible To

Camp director

 ## Camp Goals

This job description should include specific responsibilities that reflect the goals of the camp and the goals of camper development. For examples, see pages 8-9.

General Responsibilities

To drive camp vehicle in appropriate manner for camper and/or staff transportation, and to run errands as needed.

Specific Responsibilities

1. Participate in staff training and teach staff about regulations pertaining to camp vehicles.
2. Be able to operate each vehicle that might be driven.
3. Assist in coordinating driving schedule with the office manager, health care supervisor, program directors, and camp director.
4. Teach and monitor proper use of seat-belts, safe loading and unloading, proper behavior in the vehicle, and other aspects of vehicle safety.
5. Clean and maintain vehicles.

6. Coordinate vehicle repairs with maintenance supervisor.
7. Keep records on vehicle maintenance and mileage.
8. Check vehicles before and after each trip for gas, oil, tire pressure and damage, etc.
9. Keep records on all trips (e.g., mileage, number of participants, destination, time of departure and arrival, etc.)
10. Submit orders for supplies to maintenance supervisor.
11. Maintain each vehicle with complete first aid kit, current fire extinguisher, reflectors, and other safety equipment.
12. Be familiar with and follow procedures for reporting accidents, injuries, incidents, safety checks, backing up, loading and unloading, and vehicle break-down.
13. Be familiar with any health problems of campers and staff who are transported.
14. Conduct initial and end-of-season inventory of supplies and equipment.
15. Help pack all supplies at end of season.
16. Evaluate current season and make recommendations for following season.
17. These are not the only duties to be performed. Some duties may be reassigned and other duties may be assigned as required.

Essential Functions

This job description should also identify the essential functions of the job, including any physical, cognitive, visual, auditory, and other abilities essential to fulfilling the job. See pages 9-13 for an explanation of how to determine "essential functions," and for examples of those functions. Also see page 11 for examples of particular considerations for specific jobs to keep in mind when identifying essential functions.

Health Care Manager/ Registered Nurse

Desired Qualifications

- Licensed (in the appropriate state) as a registered nurse (or other appropriate training as approved by the camp physician)
- Experience with children and young adults desirable
- Ability to originate, update, and/or monitor health care, maintain records, and implement the health care plan
- Current CPR and first aid certifications
- Desire to work and live in a camp community

Responsible To

Camp director

 ## Camp Goals

This job description should include specific responsibilities that reflect the position's role in carrying out the goals of the camp and the goals of camper development. For examples, see pages 8-9.

General Responsibilities

To be the health manager for the camp; supervise health and cleanliness standards; work with camp director and staff; and help provide adequate physical health conditions for all.

Specific Responsibilities

1. Ensure each staff member and camper has on file a *health history and examination form*, as required.
2. Set up system for health screening for arriving campers and staff, as well as a system for health screening for trips out-of-camp.
3. Conduct inventory of supplies and place orders when necessary, ensuring timely arrival of supplies.

4. Establish and follow appropriate medical routines including recordkeeping in the daily medical log, disposal of medical waste, managing and safeguarding medications, and utilizing approved standing orders.
5. Coordinate coverage of the health center.
6. Post hours for daily medications and health call.
7. Make appointments, when necessary, with medical/dental personnel in the community.
8. Check and issue first-aid kits.
9. Participate in and lead specific areas of staff training pertaining to camp health and safety, CPR, first aid, and use of universal precautions for infection control.
10. Keep accident/incident reports that can be used for risk-management assessment.
11. Prepare a summary and evaluation of the camp season including inventories, staff evaluations, camper reports on health problems, and make recommendations for the following season.
12. Monitor health of all staff including kitchen staff.
13. Monitor/evaluate camp procedures, facilities, and conditions and suggest modifications that would create more healthful conditions in the camp.
14. These are not the only duties to be performed. Some duties may be reassigned and other duties may be assigned as required.

 Essential Functions

This job description should also identify the essential functions of the job, including any physical, cognitive, visual, auditory, and other abilities essential to fulfilling the job. See pages 9-13 for an explanation of how to determine "essential functions," and for examples of those functions. Also see page 11 for examples of particular considerations for specific jobs to keep in mind when identifying essential functions.

Adventure/Ropes Course Program Director

Desired Qualifications

- Training and experience with adventure/ropes course programs (must be documented); prefer someone highly experienced
- Current CPR and first aid certifications
- Ability to coordinate an adventure/ropes course program using a course designed for camp
- Ability to maintain course in excellent working condition
- Ability to supervise program assistants and make scheduling assignments
- Desire and ability to work with children outdoors
- Ability to relate to one's peer group
- Ability to accept guidance and supervision
- Good character, integrity, and adaptability
- Enthusiasm, sense of humor, patience, and self-control
- College student or at least 19 years of age

Responsible To

Camp director

 ## Camp Goals

This job description should include specific responsibilities that reflect the goals of the camp and the goals of camper development. For examples, see pages 8-9.

General Responsibility

To plan, direct, and supervise camp's adventure/ropes course program.

Specific Responsibilities

1. Set up adventure/ropes course prior to and during staff training.

2. Teach staff their responsibilities in activity area during staff training.
3. Teach and monitor proper use of equipment.
4. Conduct initial and end-of-season inventory, and store equipment for safety.
5. Check equipment and make (or file for) repairs.
6. Conduct daily check of equipment for safety, cleanliness, and good repair.
7. Write (with the help of activity assistants) and check lesson plans for all activities.
8. Keep records on all participants; help them progress from beginner to advanced levels.
9. Follow standard rules applicable to ropes course, rappelling, etc.
10. Submit orders for equipment and/or supplies when needed, ensuring timely arrival of materials.
11. Assist in packing all materials and supplies when season ends.
12. Evaluate current season and make recommendations for equipment, supplies, and program for following season.
13. These are not the only duties to be performed. Some duties may be reassigned and other duties may be assigned as required.

Essential Functions

This job description should also identify the essential functions of the job, including any physical, cognitive, visual, auditory, and other abilities essential to fulfilling the job. See pages 9-13 for an explanation of how to determine the "essential functions," and for examples of those functions. Also see page 11 for examples of particular considerations for specific jobs to keep in mind when writing essential functions.

Athletic Programs Director

Desired Qualifications

- Training and experience in athletic activities (must be documented); physical education degree preferred
- Current CPR and first aid certifications
- Ability to supervise program assistants and make scheduling assignments
- Ability to coordinate multi-faceted athletic program of teaching skills, setting up intramural and intercamp teams
- Knowledge and skills in officiating team and individual sports and the ability to teach these skills to staff and campers of all ages
- Ability to maintain athletic facilities
- Desire and ability to work with children outdoors
- Ability to relate to one's peer group
- Ability to accept guidance and supervision
- Good character, integrity, and adaptability
- Enthusiasm, sense of humor, patience, and self-control
- College student or at least 19 years of age

Responsible To

Camp director

 ## Camp Goals

This job description should include specific responsibilities that reflect the goals of the camp and the goals of camper development. For examples, see pages 8-9.

General Responsibility

To plan, direct, and supervise camp's athletic programs.

Specific Responsibilities

1. Set up athletic areas during staff training.
2. Teach staff their responsibilities in activity during staff training.
3. Teach and monitor proper use of equipment.

4. Conduct initial and end-of-season inventory, and store equipment for safety.
5. Check equipment and make (or file for) repairs.
6. Conduct daily check of program area(s) and equipment for safety, cleanliness, and good repair.
7. Write (with the help of activity assistants) and check all lesson plans.
8. Keep records on all participants; help them progress from beginner to advanced levels.
9. Plan and coordinate special athletic events including intercamp trips for camp teams, *Olympic Day, College Day,* and *Color Day.*
10. Submit orders for equipment and/or supplies, ensuring timely arrival of materials.
11. Assist in packing all materials and supplies at end of season.
12. Evaluate current season and make suggestions for following season.
13. These are not the only duties to be performed. Some duties may be reassigned and other duties may be assigned as required.

 ## Essential Functions

This job description should also identify the essential functions of the job, including any physical, cognitive, visual, auditory, and other abilities essential to fulfilling the job. See pages 9-13 for an explanation of how to determine the "essential functions," and for examples of those functions. Also see page 11 for examples of particular considerations for specific jobs to keep in mind when writing essential functions.

Bicycle Tripping Program Director

Desired Qualifications

- Training and experience in bicycle tripping activities (must be documented)
- Basic knowledge of bicycle repairs and riding skills, and ability to teach these skills to staff and campers of all ages
- Ability to supervise program assistants and make scheduling assignments
- Current CPR and first aid certifications
- Ability to set up a demonstration area and establish a program to teach skills
- Desire and ability to work with children outdoors
- Ability to relate to one's peer group
- Ability to accept guidance and supervision
- Good character, integrity, and adaptability
- Enthusiasm, sense of humor, patience, and self-control
- College student or at least 19 years of age

Responsible To

Camp director

 ## Camp Goals

This job description should include specific responsibilities that reflect the goals of the camp and the goals of camper development. For examples, see pages 8-9.

General Responsibility

To plan, direct, and supervise camp's bicycle tripping program.

Specific Responsibilities

1. Set up bicycle storage area during staff training.
2. Teach staff their responsibilities in activity during staff training.
3. Teach and monitor proper use of equipment.

4. Conduct initial and end-of-season inventory, and store equipment for safety.
5. Check equipment and make (or file for) repairs.
6. Conduct daily check of program area and equipment for safety, cleanliness, and good repair.
7. Write (with help of activity assistants) and check all lesson plans.
8. Keep records on all participants; help them progress from beginner to advanced levels.
9. Plan trips based on camper's skills.
10. Teach campers to do simple bicycle repairs.
11. Submit orders for equipment and/or supplies when needed, ensuring timely arrival of materials.
12. Assist in packing all equipment and supplies at end of season.
13. Evaluate current season and make recommendations for following season.
14. These are not the only duties to be performed. Some duties may be reassigned and other duties may be assigned as required.

 Essential Functions

This job description should also identify the essential functions of the job, including any physical, cognitive, visual, auditory, and other abilities essential to fulfilling the job. See pages 9-13 for an explanation of how to determine the "essential functions," and for examples of those functions. Also see page 11 for examples of particular considerations for specific jobs to keep in mind when writing essential functions.

This job description could easily be altered to fit a specific arts program director position.

Creative Arts Program Director

Desired Qualifications

- Training and experience in creative arts (documented)
- Ability to teach creative skills in at least one of the arts areas
- Ability to set up demonstration area and program, and to teach skills to staff and campers of all ages
- Ability to supervise staff, make scheduling assignments, and order supplies and equipment
- Desire and ability to work with children outdoors
- Ability to relate to one's peer group
- Ability to accept guidance and supervision
- Good character, integrity, and ability to adapt to camp setting
- Enthusiasm, sense of humor, patience, and self-control
- College student or at least 19 years of age

Responsible To

Camp director

Camp Goals

This job description should include specific responsibilities that reflect the goals of the camp and the goals of camper development. For examples, see pages 8-9.

General Responsibility

To plan, direct, and supervise camp's creative arts program including drama, crafts, arts, jewelry, and ceramics.

Specific Responsibilities

1. Set up creative arts areas during staff training.
2. Teach staff their responsibilities in activities during staff training.
3. Teach and monitor proper use of equipment.

4. Conduct initial and end-of-season inventory, and store equipment for safety.
5. Create check-out and return system for craft supplies.
6. Check equipment and make (or file for) repairs.
7. Conduct daily check of program area and equipment for safety, cleanliness, and good repair.
8. Write (with help of activity assistants) and check all lesson plans for creative arts programming.
9. Keep records on all participants; help them progress from beginner to advanced levels.
10. Plan and direct camp-wide drama programs including plays, puppet shows, talent shows, welcome skits, skit nights, etc.
11. Assist with overall camp activities regarding creative arts.
12. Submit orders for equipment and supplies when needed, ensuring timely arrival of materials.
13. Assist in packing all materials and supplies at end of season.
14. Evaluate current season and make recommendations for equipment, supplies, and program for following season.
15. These are not the only duties to be performed. Some duties may be reassigned and other duties may be assigned as required.

▶ **Essential Functions**

This job description should also identify the essential functions of the job, including any physical, cognitive, visual, auditory, and other abilities essential to fulfilling the job. See pages 9-13 for an explanation of how to determine the "essential functions," and for examples of those functions. Also see page 11 for examples of particular considerations for specific jobs to keep in mind when writing essential functions.

Environmental Education/ Outdoor Living Skills Program Director

Desired Qualifications

- Training and experience in environmental education and outdoor living skill activities (must be documented); ACA OLS training perferred
- Current first aid and CPR certifications
- Ability to set up demonstration area and program, and to teach skills to staff and campers of all ages
- Ability to supervise assistants and make scheduling assignments
- Desire and ability to work with children outdoors
- Ability to relate to one's peer group
- Ability to accept guidance and supervision
- Good character, integrity, and adaptability
- Enthusiasm, sense of humor, patience, and self-control
- College student or at least 19 years of age

Responsible To

Camp director

 ## Camp Goals

This job description should include specific responsibilities that reflect the goals of the camp and the goals of camper development. For examples, see pages 8-9.

General Responsibilities

To plan, direct, and supervise camp's environmental education and outdoor living skills program.

Specific Responsibilities

1. Set up nature center and outdoor skills area(s) during staff training.

2. Teach staff their responsibilities in activity during staff training.
3. Teach and monitor proper use of equipment.
4. Conduct initial and end-of-season inventory, and store equipment for safety.
5. Check equipment and make (or file for) repairs.
6. Conduct daily check of program area and equipment for safety, cleanliness, and good repair.
7. Write (with help of activity assistants) lesson plans that will foster participants' outdoor living skills and environmental sensitivity. Check all lesson plans.
8. Keep records on all participants; help them progress from beginner to advanced levels.
9. Work with overnight camping director and head counselors.
10. Plan trips based on campers' skills.
11. Plan cabin cookouts with head counselors.
12. Submit orders for equipment and supplies when needed, ensuring timely arrival of materials.
13. Assist in packing all materials and supplies at end of season.
14. Evaluate current seasons and make recommendations for equipment, supplies, and program for following season.
15. These are not the only duties to be performed. Some duties may be reassigned and other duties may be assigned as required.

 ## Essential Functions

This job description should also identify the essential functions of the job, including any physical, cognitive, visual, auditory, and other abilities essential to fulfilling the job. See pages 9-13 for an explanation of how to determine the "essential functions," and for examples of those functions. Also see page 11 for examples of particular considerations for specific jobs to keep in mind when writing essential functions.

Gymnastics Program Director

Desired Qualifications

- Training and experience in gymnastics (must be documented); prefer college team member or instructor
- Ability to teach gymnastics to campers of all ages
- Ability to set up gymnastic area involving the horse, uneven and parallel bars, and balance beam
- Ability to supervise program assistants and make scheduling assignments
- Ability to organize, select, and coach an intercamp gymnastic team
- Desire and ability to work with children outdoors
- Ability to relate to one's peer group
- Ability to accept guidance and supervision
- Good character, integrity, and adaptability
- Enthusiasm, sense of humor, patience, and self-control
- College student or at least 19 years of age

Responsible to

Camp director

Camp Goals

This job description should include specific responsibilities that reflect the goals of the camp and the goals of camper development. For examples, see pages 8-9.

General Responsibilities

To plan, direct, and supervise camp's gymnastics program.

Specific Responsibilities

1. Set up gymnastic area during staff training.
2. Teach staff their responsibilities in activity during staff training.
3. Train, supervise, and schedule program assistant(s).

4. Teach and monitor proper use of equipment.
5. Conduct initial and end-of-season inventory, and store equipment for safety.
6. Check equipment and make (or file for) repairs.
7. Conduct daily check of equipment for safety, cleanliness, and good repair.
8. Write (with help of program assistants) and check all lesson plans.
9. Keep records on all participants; help them progress from beginner to advanced levels.
10. Set up a gymnastic exhibition.
11. Submit orders for equipment and supplies when needed, ensuring timely arrival of materials.
12. Assist in packing all materials and supplies at end of season.
13. Evaluate current season and make suggestions for following season.
14. These are not the only duties to be performed. Some duties may be reassigned and other duties may be assigned as required.

Essential Functions

This job description should also identify the essential functions of the job, including any physical, cognitive, visual, auditory, and other abilities essential to fulfilling the job. See pages 9-13 for an explanation of how to determine the "essential functions," and for examples of those functions. Also see page 11 for examples of particular considerations for specific jobs to keep in mind when writing essential functions.

Pool Director

Desired Qualifications

- Training and experience in pool and swimming activities
- Current certifications appropriate to position (i.e., water safety instructor, lifeguarding, etc.)
- Current CPR and first aid certifications
- Knowledge of pool management
- Ability to schedule and supervise staff
- Desire and ability to work with children outdoors
- Ability to relate to one's peer group
- Ability to accept guidance and supervision
- Good character, integrity, and adaptability
- Enthusiasm, sense of humor, patience, and self-control
- College student or at least 19 years of age

Responsible To

Camp director

Camp Goals

This job description should include specific responsibilities that reflect the goals of the camp and the goals of camper development. For examples, see pages 8-9.

General Responsibilities

To plan, direct, and supervise camp's pool program.

Specific Responsibilities

1. Set up pool area during staff training.
2. Teach staff their responsibilities in activity during staff training.
3. Teach and monitor proper use of equipment.
4. Conduct initial and end-of-season inventory, and store equipment for safety.
5. Check equipment and make (or file for) repairs.
6. Conduct daily check of equipment in area for safety, cleanliness, and good repair.

7. Evaluate aquatic abilities of staff and campers.
8. Write (with help of activity assistants) lesson plans that foster participants' aquatic skills. Check all lesson plans.
9. Keep records on all participants; help them progress from beginner to advanced levels.
10. Award recognition and participation certificates to campers, when earned.
11. Work with others during special events (i.e., swim meets, early morning swims, etc.).
12. Submit orders for equipment and supplies when needed, ensuring timely arrival of materials.
13. Assist in packing all materials and supplies at end of season.
14. Evaluate current season and make suggestions for following season.
15. These are not the only duties to be performed. Some duties may be reassigned and other duties may be assigned as required.

 Essential Functions

This job description should also identify the essential functions of the job, including any physical, cognitive, visual, auditory, and other abilities essential to fulfilling the job. See pages 9-13 for an explanation of how to determine the "essential functions," and for examples of those functions. Also see page 11 for examples of particular considerations for specific jobs to keep in mind when writing essential functions.

Waterfront Director

Desired Qualifications

- Training and experience in waterfront activities and management
- Current smallcraft instructor's certification
- Current lifeguarding certification
- Current CPR and first aid certifications
- Ability to schedule and supervise staff
- Desire and ability to work with children outdoors
- Ability to relate to one's peer group
- Ability to accept guidance and supervision
- Good character, integrity, and adaptability
- Enthusiasm, sense of humor, patience, and self-control
- College student or at least 19 years of age

Responsible To

Camp director

 ## Camp Goals

This job description should include specific responsibilities that reflect the goals of the camp and the goals of camper development. For examples, see pages 8-9.

General Responsibility

To plan, direct, and supervise camp's waterfront program.

Specific Responsibilities

1. Set up lake or waterfront area during staff training.
2. Teach staff their responsibilities in activity during staff training.
3. Teach and monitor proper use of equipment.
4. Conduct initial and end-of-season inventory, and store equipment for safety.
5. Check equipment and make (or file for) repairs.
6. Conduct daily check of area and equipment for safety, cleanliness, and good repair.

7. Write (with help of activity assistants) and check all lesson plans to make sure they foster participants' aquatic skills.

8. Keep records on all participants; help them progress from beginner to advanced levels.

9. Award recognition and participation certificates to campers, when earned.

10. Evaluate aquatics abilities of staff and campers.

11. Plan and work with others during special events (i.e., college days for lake activities).

12. Submit orders for equipment and supplies when needed, ensuring timely arrival of materials.

13. Assist in packing all materials and supplies at end of season.

14. Evaluate current season and make suggestions for following season.

15. These are not the only duties to be performed. Some duties may be reassigned and other duties may be assigned as required.

 Essential Functions

This job description should also identify the essential functions of the job, including any physical, cognitive, visual, auditory, and other abilities essential to fulfilling the job. See pages 9-13 for an explanation of how to determine the "essential functions," and for examples of those functions. Also see page 11 for examples of particular considerations for specific jobs to keep in mind when writing essential functions.

Activity Assistant

This job description could easily be altered to fit almost any specific activity counselor position.

Desired Qualifications

- Desire and ability to work with children outdoors
- Ability to relate to one's peer group
- Ability to accept guidance and supervision
- Ability to teach skills to other staff members and campers of all ages
- Specialized training in activity area
- Good character, integrity, adaptability, enthusiasm, sense of humor, patience, and self-control
- High school graduate or equivalent, or at least 18 years of age

Responsible To

Activity director

Camp Goals

This job description should include specific responsibilities that reflect the goals of the camp and the goals of camper development. For examples, see pages 8-9.

General Responsibility

To assist in teaching and coordinating a skill or activity, maintaining standards that lead to a quality program.

Specific Responsibilities

1. Work with activity head during staff training to set up area and program for campers.
2. Assist in coordinating specialization with other camp activities and plans.
3. Write lesson plans, with help of activity head, for each program session.
4. Participate in weekly program evaluations conducted by staff within the specific activity.
5. Conduct daily check of program area and equipment for safety, cleanliness, and good repair.

6. Submit orders for equipment and supplies when needed, with approval of activity head, ensuring timely arrival of materials.

7. Teach and monitor proper use of equipment.

8. Keep records on participant's progress; help them progress from beginner to advanced levels.

9. Assist in conducting initial and end-of-season inventory, storing, and keeping equipment in good condition.

10. Assist in packing all materials and supplies when season ends.

11. Evaluate current season and make recommendations for equipment, supplies, and program for following season.

12. These are not the only duties to be performed. Some duties may be reassigned and other duties may be assigned as required.

 ## Essential Functions

This job description should also identify the essential functions of the job, including any physical, cognitive, visual, auditory, and other abilities essential to fulfilling the job. See pages 9-13 for an explanation of how to determine "essential functions," and for examples of those functions. Also see page 11 for examples of particular considerations for specific jobs to keep in mind when writing essential functions.

Archery Counselor

This job description could easily be altered to fit the riflery counselor position.

Desired Qualifications

- Training and experience in archery (documented)
- Ability to teach archery to campers of all ages
- Ability to set up a range, order and repair equipment
- Ability to organize, select, and coach an intercamp archery team
- Desire and ability to work with children outdoors
- Ability to relate to one's peer group
- Ability to accept guidance and supervision
- Good character, integrity, and adaptability
- Enthusiasm, sense of humor, patience, and self-control
- High school graduate or equivalent, or at least 18 years of age

Responsible To

Athletic director

Camp Goals

This job description should include specific responsibilities that reflect the goals of the camp and the goals of camper development. For examples, see pages 8-9.

General Responsibility

To teach and help coordinate camp's archery program, maintaining standards that lead to a quality program.

Specific Responsibilities

1. Work with athletic director during staff training to set up area and program for campers.
2. Assist in coordinating specialization with other camp activities and plans.
3. Write lesson plans, with help of athletic director, that will foster participant's archery skills.
4. Participate in weekly staff meetings.

5. Assist in conducting daily check of equipment in program area for safety, cleanliness, and good repair.
6. Submit orders for equipment and supplies when needed, with approval of athletic director, ensuring timely arrival of materials.
7. Teach and monitor proper use of equipment.
8. Keep records on participant's progress; help them progress from beginner to advanced levels.
9. Assist in conducting initial and end-of-season inventory, storing, and keeping equipment in good condition.
10. Assist in packing materials and supplies for following season.
11. Evaluate current season and make suggestions for following season.
12. These are not the only duties to be performed. Some duties may be reassigned and other duties may be assigned as required.

 ## Essential Functions

This job description should also identify the essential functions of the job, including any physical, cognitive, visual, auditory, and other abilities essential to fulfilling the job. See pages 9-13 for an explanation of how to determine "essential functions," and for examples of those functions. Also see page 11 for examples of particular considerations for specific jobs to keep in mind when writing essential functions.

Athletic Counselor

This job description could easily be altered to fit any number of specific sports counselor positions.

Desired Qualifications

- Training and experience in athletic activities (documented); junior- or senior-level physical education or recreation major preferred
- Ability to teach proper sports skills to campers of all ages
- Current CPR and first aid certifications
- Knowledge of team sports and ability to teach and referee
- Desire and ability to work with children outdoors
- Ability to relate to one's peer group
- Ability to accept guidance and supervision
- Good character, integrity, and adaptability
- Enthusiasm, sense of humor, patience, and self-control
- High school graduate or equivalent, or at least 18 years of age

Responsible To

Athletic director

 ## Camp Goals

This job description should include specific responsibilities that reflect the goals of the camp and the goals of camper development. For examples, see pages 8-9.

General Responsibility

To teach and help coordinate the camp's athletic program, and to help maintain standards that lead to a quality program.

Specific Responsibilities

1. Assist athletic director in setting up camp's sports area(s).
2. Assist in total athletic program.
3. Assist in checking equipment and making (or filing for) repairs.
4. Assist in conducting initial and end-of-season inventory, storing, and keeping equipment in good condition.

5. Assist in coordinating specialty with other camp activities and plans.
6. Assist in teaching staff their responsibilities in activity during staff training.
7. Write lesson plans, with help of athletic director, that foster participants' athletic skills.
8. Keep records on all participants; help them progress from beginner to advanced levels.
9. Select and work with intercamp teams.
10. Conduct daily check of facilities and equipment in program area for safety, cleanliness, and good repair.
11. Submit orders for equipment and supplies when needed, with approval of athletic director, ensuring timely arrival of materials
12. Teach and monitor proper use of equipment.
13. Assist in packing all materials and supplies at end of season.
14. Evaluate current season and make recommendations for following season.
15. These are not the only duties to be performed. Some duties may be reassigned and other duties may be assigned as required.

▶ Essential Functions

This job description should also identify the essential functions of the job, including any physical, cognitive, visual, auditory, and other abilities essential to fulfilling the job. See pages 9-13 for an explanation of how to determine "essential functions," and for examples of those functions. Also see page 11 for examples of particular considerations for specific jobs to keep in mind when writing essential functions.

Ceramics Counselor

This job description could easily be altered to fit almost any creative arts program counselor position.

Desired Qualifications

- Training and experience in ceramics (documented)
- Ability to teach creative-ceramics skills to campers of all ages
- Basic knowledge of how to use and care for a kiln and other ceramics equipment
- Knowledge to set up a demonstration area and program
- Desire and ability to work with children outdoors
- Ability to relate to one's peer group
- Ability to accept guidance and supervision
- Good character, integrity, and adaptability
- Enthusiasm, sense of humor, patience, and self-control
- High school graduate or equivalent, or at least 18 years of age

Responsible To

Creative arts program director

Camp Goals

This job description should include specific responsibilities that reflect the goals of the camp and the goals of camper development. For examples, see pages 8-9.

General Responsibility

To teach and help coordinate camp's ceramics program, and help maintain standards that lead to a quality program.

Specific Responsibilities

1. Set up ceramics area during staff training.
2. Check kilns and other equipment and file for repairs.
3. Assist in conducting initial and end-of-season inventory, storing, and keeping equipment in good condition.
4. Assist in coordinating specialization with other camp activities.

5. Assist in teaching staff their responsibilities in activity during staff training.
6. Write lesson plans, with help of creative arts program director, that foster participants' ceramics skills.
7. Keep records on all participants; help them progress from beginner to advanced levels.
8. Conduct daily check of ceramics program area and equipment for safety, cleanliness, and good repair.
9. Submit orders for equipment and supplies when needed, with approval of creative arts program director, ensuring timely arrival of materials.
10. Teach and monitor proper use of equipment.
11. Assist in packing all materials and supplies at end of season.
12. Evaluate current season and make recommendations for equipment, supplies, and program for following season.
13. These are not the only duties to be performed. Some duties may be reassigned and other duties may be assigned as required.

 ## Essential Functions

This job description should also identify the essential functions of the job, including any physical, cognitive, visual, auditory, and other abilities essential to fulfilling the job. See pages 9-13 for an explanation of how to determine "essential functions," and for examples of those functions. Also see page 11 for examples of particular considerations for specific jobs to keep in mind when writing essential functions.

Creative Writing/ Newspaper Counselor

Desired Qualifications

- Ability to teach writing and newspaper skills to campers of all ages
- Desire and ability to work with children outdoors
- Ability to relate to one's peer group
- Ability to accept guidance and supervision
- Good character, integrity, and ability to adapt
- Enthusiasm, sense of humor, patience, and self-control
- Some typing and word-processing skills
- Self-motivation
- High school graduate or equivalent, or at least 18 years of age

Responsible To

Creative arts program director

Camp Goals

This job description should include specific responsibilities that reflect the goals of the camp and the goals of camper development. For examples, see pages 8-9.

General Responsibility

To teach and help coordinate camp's writing program and camp newspaper, and help maintain standards that lead to a quality program.

Specific Responsibilities

1. Assist in setting up activity area during staff training; unpack library books.
2. Assist in checking equipment and making (or filing for) repairs.
3. Assist in conducting initial and end-of-season inventory, storing, and keeping equipment in good condition.

4. Assist in coordinating specialization with other camp activities.

5. Assist in teaching staff their responsibilities in activity during staff training.

6. Write lesson plans, with help of creative arts program director, that foster participants' writing skills.

7. Coordinate and edit at least three camper newspapers.

8. Keep records on all participants; help them progress from beginner to advanced levels.

9. Conduct daily check of equipment in program area for safety, cleanliness, and good repair.

10. Submit orders for equipment and supplies when needed, with approval of creative arts program director, ensuring timely arrival of materials.

11. Teach and monitor proper use of equipment.

12. Assist in packing all materials and supplies at end of season.

13. Evaluate current season and make suggestions for following season.

14. These are not the only duties to be performed. Some duties may be reassigned and other duties may be assigned as required.

▶ **Essential Functions**

This job description should also identify the essential functions of the job, including any physical, cognitive, visual, auditory, and other abilities essential to fulfilling the job. See pages 9-13 for an explanation of how to determine "essential functions," and for examples of those functions. Also see page 11 for examples of particular considerations for specific jobs to keep in mind when writing essential functions.

Dance Counselor

Desired Qualifications

- Training and experience in dance — jazz, modern, creative, ballet (documented)
- Ability to teach dance skills to campers of all ages
- Desire and ability to work with children outdoors
- Ability to relate to one's peer group
- Ability to accept guidance and supervision
- Good character, integrity, and adaptability
- Enthusiasm, sense of humor, patience, and self-control
- High school graduate or equivalent, or at least 18 years of age

Responsible To

Creative arts program director

Camp Goals

This job description should include specific responsibilities that reflect the goals of the camp and the goals of camper development. For examples, see pages 8-9.

General Responsibilities

To teach and help coordinate camp's dance program, and help maintain standards that lead to a quality program.

Specific Responsibilities

1. Check equipment on hand.
2. Assist in conducting initial and end-of-season inventory, storing, and keeping equipment in good condition.
3. Assist in coordinating specialization with other camp activities.
4. Clean, set up, and maintain the dance facility.
5. Assist in teaching staff their responsibilities in activity during staff training.
6. Write lesson plans, with help of creative arts program director, that foster participants' dancing skills.

7. Assist drama staff, cabin groups, etc., when requested.
8. Keep records on all participants; help them progress from beginner to advanced levels.
9. Submit orders for equipment and supplies when needed, with approval of creative arts program director, ensuring timely arrival of materials.
10. Teach and monitor proper use of equipment.
11. Assist in packing all materials and supplies at end of season.
12. Evaluate current season and make suggestions for following season.
13. These are not the only duties to be performed. Some duties may be reassigned and other duties may be assigned as required.

 Essential Functions

This job description should also identify the essential functions of the job, including any physical, cognitive, visual, auditory, and other abilities essential to fulfilling the job. See pages 9-13 for an explanation of how to determine "essential functions," and for examples of those functions. Also see page 11 for examples of particular considerations for specific jobs to keep in mind when writing essential functions.

Song Leader

This job description may exist as a position on its own, but may become part of another position in camp.

Desired Qualifications

- Training and experience in song-leading
- Knowledge of camp songs and ability to lead
- Skill as an accompanist — piano, guitar, accordion, etc.
- Desire and ability to work with children outdoors
- Ability to relate to one's peer group
- Ability to accept guidance and supervision
- Good character, integrity, and adaptability
- Enthusiasm, sense of humor, patience, and self-control
- High school graduate or equivalent, or at least 18 years of age

Responsible To

Creative arts program director

 ## Camp Goals

This job description should include specific responsibilities that reflect the goals of the camp and the goals of camper development. For examples, see pages 8-9.

General Responsibilities

To take charge of camp's music and singing program.

Specific Responsibilities

1. Familiarize self with camp songs to prepare for camp season.
2. Teach songs and lead singing during staff training.
3. Assist in coordinating specialization with other camp activities.
4. Assist in conducting initial and end-of-season inventory, storing, and keeping equipment in good condition.
5. Write lesson plans, with help of creative arts program director, that foster the participants' singing.
6. Coordinate camp's songfest and organize camp chorus.

7. Keep records on all participants; help them progress from beginner to advanced levels.
8. Assist drama staff when needed.
9. Submit orders for equipment and supplies when needed, with approval of creative arts program director, ensuring timely arrival of materials.
10. Teach and monitor proper use of equipment.
11. Assist in packing all materials and supplies at end of season.
12. Evaluate current season and make suggestions for following season.
13. These are not the only duties to be performed. Some duties may be reassigned and other duties may be assigned as required.

Essential Functions

This job description should also identify the essential functions of the job, including any physical, cognitive, visual, auditory, and other abilities essential to fulfilling the job. See pages 9-13 for an explanation of how to determine "essential functions," and for examples of those functions. Also see page 11 for examples of particular considerations for specific jobs to keep in mind when writing essential functions.

Waterfront Staff

Desired Qualifications

- Training and experience in waterfront activities
- Current water safety instructor's certification
- Current lifeguarding, smallcraft (lake position), and other certifications as appropriate to position
- Current CPR and first aid certifications
- Desire and ability to work with children outdoors
- Ability to relate to one's peer group
- Ability to accept guidance and supervision
- Good character, integrity, and adaptability
- Enthusiasm, sense of humor, patience, and self-control
- High school graduate or equivalent, or at least 18 years of age

Responsible To

Waterfront director

 ## Camp Goals

This job description should include specific responsibilities that reflect the goals of the camp and the goals of camper development. For examples, see pages 8-9.

General Responsibilities

To teach and help coordinate camp's waterfront and swimming activities, and help maintain standards that lead to a quality program.

Specific Responsibilities

1. Assist in checking equipment and making (or filing for) repairs.
2. Assist in conducting initial and end-of-season inventory, storing, and keeping equipment in good condition.
3. Assist in coordinating specialization with other camp activities.

4. During staff training, work with aquatics director to set up waterfront area and teach staff their responsibilities in activity.
5. Write lesson plans, with help of waterfront director, that foster participants' aquatic skills.
6. Keep records on all participants; help them progress from beginner to advanced levels.
7. Award recognition and participation certificates to campers, when earned.
8. Conduct daily check of equipment in area for safety, cleanliness, and good repair.
9. Submit orders for equipment and supplies when needed, with approval of waterfront director, ensuring timely arrival of materials.
10. Teach and monitor proper use of equipment.
11. Assist in packing all materials and supplies at end of season.
12. Evaluate current season and make suggestions for following season.
13. These are not the only duties to be performed. Some duties may be reassigned and other duties may be assigned as required.

▶ ### Essential Functions

This job description should also identify the essential functions of the job, including any physical, cognitive, visual, auditory, and other abilities essential to fulfilling the job. See pages 9-13 for an explanation of how to determine "essential functions," and for examples of those functions. Also see page 11 for examples of particular considerations for specific jobs to keep in mind when writing essential functions.

Head Counselor/ Unit Leader

Desired Qualifications

- Previous camp staff experience
- Current CPR and first aid certifications
- Desire and ability to work with children and adults in camp setting
- Ability to creatively schedule programs, facilities, and staff
- Ability and experience in supervising staff and campers
- College student of at least 21 years of age

Responsible To

Camp director

 ### Camp Goals

This job description should include specific responsibilities that reflect the goals of the camp and the goals of camper development. For examples, see pages 8-9.

General Responsibility

To train staff in their responsibilities.

Specific Responsibilities

1. Prior to camp, contact staff who will be assigned to your unit.
2. During staff training, teach staff their responsibilities.

General Responsibility

To supervise staff and program.

Specific Responsibilities

1. Awaken campers and staff on time, know and communicate proper attire for the day and activity.
2. Conduct or delegate responsibility for inspection of cabins and areas.
3. Visit cabins regularly during the day as a supervisory tool, but also to provide opportunity to get to know campers and staff.
4. Be knowledgeable about the eating habits and diets of campers.
5. Monitor counselor and camper assignments for the day.
6. Together with unit staff and campers, plan and execute the evening program.
7. Correct or reprimand other staff as soon as possible (in private), for actions that put health and safety of a camper at risk.
8. Monitor that activity counselors take responsibility for cabin groups at appropriate times.
9. Check with and excuse counselors from the group at campers' curfew and after campers are in bed.
10. In the event an activity counselor is ill or their employment is terminated, lead the activity temporarily.

General Responsibility

To counsel staff and campers.

Specific Responsibilities

1. Be responsible for the welfare of each individual in the unit and do all possible to solve problems.
2. Inform director of any camper or staff problems.
3. With help of other staff, evaluate the elective choices of campers.
4. Assist those campers and staff who may need help fitting into camp atmosphere.
5. Help ensure morale of staff by monitoring that staff get enough rest, time and days off, and that recreational opportunities are available to them.
6. As appropriate, speak with campers' parents.

General Responsibility

To evaluate the program.

Specific Responsibilities

1. Monitor food service and eating habits.
2. Discuss with director the performance of all staff.
3. Evaluate division or unit staff, and assist staff in setting objectives so that they can meet the expectation of activity supervisors.
4. Formally evaluate staff at least twice a season, conducting other evaluations as necessary.
5. Supervise and check the writing of all final staff reports as they pertain to campers and program.
6. Assist in evaluating the entire camp operation with suggestions for the following season.
7. These are not the only duties to be performed. Some duties may be reassigned and other duties may be assigned as required.

 ## Essential Functions

This job description should also identify the essential functions of the job, including any physical, cognitive, visual, auditory, and other abilities essential to fulfilling the job. See pages 9-13 for an explanation of how to determine "essential functions," and for examples of those functions. Also see page 11 for examples of particular considerations for specific jobs to keep in mind when writing essential functions.

General Counselor

Desired Qualifications

- Desire and ability to work with children outdoors
- Ability to relate to one's peer group
- Ability to accept supervision and guidance
- Ability to assist in teaching an activity
- Good character, integrity, and adaptability
- Enthusiasm, sense of humor, patience, and self-control
- High school graduate or equivalent, or at least 18 years of age

Responsible To

Head counselor and/or camp director

Camp Goals

This job description should include specific responsibilities that reflect the goals of the camp and the goals of camper development. For examples, see pages 8-9.

General Responsibility

To identify and meet camper needs.

Specific Responsibilities

1. Learn the likes/dislikes of each participant.
2. Recognize and respond to opportunities for problem solving in the group.
3. Develop opportunities for interaction between campers and staff.
4. Provide opportunities for the group so that each individual experiences success during camp.
5. Provide opportunities for discussion of individual or group problems or concerns.
6. Help each participant meet the goals established by the camp for camper development.

General Responsibility

To carry out camp programs.

Specific Responsibilities

1. Guide cabin or unit groups and individual campers in participating successfully in all aspects of camp activities.
2. Carry out established roles for supervising camper health.
3. Carry out established roles in enforcing camp safety regulations.
4. Develop cabin or unit activity plans with participants as appropriate.
5. Supervise all assigned aspects of the campers' day including morning reveille, cabin clean-up, meal times, rest hour, evening activities, getting ready for bed, and after-hours duty as assigned.
6. Instruct campers in emergency procedures such as fire drills, evacuating the cabin, etc.
7. Help campers plan their participation in unit-wide or camp-wide programs, special events, and activities.
8. Assist in teaching or leading an activity, as assigned.

General Responsibility

To fulfill other staff administrative roles.

Specific Responsibilities

1. Prepare for and actively participate in staff training, meetings, and supervisory conferences.
2. Set a good example for campers and others including cleanliness, punctuality, sharing clean-up and chores, sportsmanship, and table manners.
3. Follow camp rules and regulations pertaining to smoking, use of alcoholic beverages, and use of drugs.
4. Encourage respect for personal property, camp equipment, and facilities.
5. Manage personal time off in accordance with camp policy.
6. Maintain good public relations with campers' parents.
7. Submit all required reports on time.
8. These are not the only duties to be performed. Some duties may be reassigned and other duties may be assigned as required.

Essential Functions

This job description should also identify the essential functions of the job, including any physical, cognitive, visual, auditory, and other abilities essential to fulfilling the job. See pages 9-13 for an explanation of how to determine "essential functions," and for examples of those functions. Also see page 11 for examples of particular considerations for specific jobs to keep in mind when writing essential functions.

Additional Duties for Day and Resident Camp Counselors

In "customizing" this job description to your day or resident camp, be aware of the following kinds of duties which may be unique to the duration of your camp day.

Day camp counselors may be required to drive vehicles for picking up and dropping off campers at their homes. This may entail using their own vehicles, participating in driver training sessions, or acquiring a special kind of drivers' license. In addition, day camp counselors will often supervise the arrival and departure of campers where there are important safety considerations. These transportation responsibilities may result in more frequent contact with campers' parents, bringing the opportunity to share information about the camper's progress and being a good ambassador for the camp.

In addition to those responsibilities listed above, *resident camp counselors* often supervise daily cabin or camp-wide clean-up chores, and have a shared responsibility to supervise the unit or cabin area after hours. They also have the responsibility to see that campers wear clean clothing and are appropriately dressed for the weather and activities of the day. Counselors may also be asked to see to it that campers write home. They bear a heavy responsibility for being aware of the health and well-being of their assigned campers.

Camp Staff Application   Form FM 10

Developed by *American Camping Association*sm

Return to:

(Please type or print)   Date of Application _____

Name _____   Social Security Number _____

Permanent Address _____   Phone _____
 Street & Number .... *City* .... *State* ... *Zip* .... *Area/Number*

School or Business Address_____   Phone _____
 Street & Number .... *City* ... *State* ... *Zip* .... *Area/Number*

Are there any reasons you may have difficulty in performing any of the essential functions of the job for which you have applied? ☐ Yes ☐ No   If so, please explain _____

_____

_____

_____

If you are hired would you desire or need housing for any person(s) other than yourself at the camp? ☐ Yes ☐ No

Education

Years	School	Major Subjects	Degree Granted

Past Employment *(List previous two summers or years.)*

Dates	Employer	Address/Phone	Nature of Work	Supervisor	Reason for Leaving

Indicate any employer you do not wish us to contact and the reason _____

_____

Camp Experience

Dates	Camp	Director	Address	Camper or Staff

References *(Give names/addresses of 3 persons [not relatives] having knowledge of your character, experience and ability.)*

Name	Address & City	Phone

What type of position do you want at camp? _____   Salary desired? _____

Dates available From _____   To _____

In the following list, put numeral "1" before those activities you can organize and teach as an expert; "2" for those activities in which you can assist in teaching; and, "3" for those which are just your hobby; "C" for those in which you have *current* certification.

Adventure/Challenge
____ Climbing/Rappelling
____ Ropes Course
____ Spelunking

Arts and Crafts
____ Basketry
____ Ceramics
____ Electronics
____ Ham Radio
____ Jewelry
____ Leather Work
____ Macrame
____ Metal Work
____ Model Rocketry
____ Nature Crafts
____ Newspaper
____ Painting
____ Photography
____ Darkroom
____ Sketching
____ Weaving
____ Woodworking

Camp Craft/Pioneering
____ Campcraft
____ OLS Program Leader
____ OLS Instructor
____ Hiking
____ Orienteering
____ Outdoor Cooking
____ Overnight
____ Mountaineering
____ Min.-Impact Camping

Dancing
____ Ballet
____ Folk
____ Social
____ Square
____ Tap
____ _____
____ _____

Dramatics
____ Creative
____ Play Directing
____ Skits and Stunts

Music
____ Lead Singing
____ Instruments (list)
____ Accordion
____ Bugle
____ Piano
____ Guitar
____ ____ ____
____ ____ ____

Nature
____ Animals
____ Astronomy
____ Birds
____ Conservation
____ Flowers
____ Forestry
____ Insects
____ Rocks and Minerals
____ Trees and Shrubs
____ Weather
____ Gardening
____ Animal Care

Sports
____ Archery
____ Archery Certification
____ Badminton
____ Baseball
____ Basketball
____ Boxing
____ Fencing
____ Fishing
____ Bait Casting
____ Fly Casting
____ Hockey
____ Informal Games
____ Ping Pong
____ Riding
____ CHA Certification
____ HSI Instructor
____ Riflery
____ NRA Instructor
____ Soccer
____ Softball
____ Tennis
____ Track and Field
____ Volleyball
____ Wrestling

Waterfront Activities
____ Canoeing/Kayaking
____ Diving
____ ARC/WSI
____ ARC/EWS
____ Basic Lifeguarding
____ BSA/Aquatic Instructor
____ ARC/Lifeguard Training
____ BSA/Lifeguard
____ YMCA/Life Guard
____ Rowing
____ Sailing
____ Scuba
____ Swimming
____ Water Skiing
____ Board Sailing
____ Rafting
____ Synchronized Swimming

Miscellaneous
____ Standard First Aid Cert.
____ Community First Aid and Safety
____ CPR
____ Responding to Emergencies
____ Auto Mechanics
____ Campfire Programs
____ Carpentry
____ Electrical
____ Evening Programs
____ Farming
____ Library
____ Plumbing
____ Shorthand
____ Storytelling
____ Word Processing
____ Worship Services
____ Language

Answer these questions <u>only</u> if applying for a position requiring driving

Do you have a valid driver's license? ☐ Yes ☐ No   State _____

Do you have current chauffeur's-type license? ☐ Yes ☐ No   Do you have a commercial driver's license? ☐ Yes ☐ No

---

What contributions do you think you can make at camp? _____
_____
_____
_____

What contribution do you think a well-run camp can make to children? _____
_____
_____
_____

Write a brief biographical sketch, including specialized training in camping, and experience or training in other fields which might have a bearing on the position(s) for which you are applying. _____
_____
_____
_____
_____
_____

Are you available for an interview? ☐ Yes ☐ No   Where? _____

I authorize investigation of all statements herein and release the camp and all others from liability in connection with same. understand that, if employed, I will be an at-will employee and that any agreement to the contrary must be in writing and signe by the director of the camp. I also understand that untrue, misleading, or omitted information herein may result in dismissa regardless of the time of discovery by the camp.

Signature _____

All statements become part of any future employee personnel files.

This form has been drafted to comply with federal employment laws; however, ACA assumes no responsibility or liability for the use of this form.

Staff Information Composite

This is an example of a form that may be kept in a prospective staff member's file to keep track of notes about the applicant, dates when referrals are requested and received, dates when materials are sent to applicant, etc.

Name _____

Phone _____

Address _____

City _____ State _____ Zip _____

Position applying for:

☐ Program Director   ☐ Activity Staff

☐ Assistant Unit Leader   ☐ Waterfront Director

☐ Camp Nurse   ☐ Waterfront Assistant

☐ Lake Personnel   ☐ Unit Leader

☐ General Counselor

Special skills/qualifications: _____

_____

Source:

☐ Request by mail   ☐ Job fair

☐ Application on file   ☐ Advertisement

☐ Request by phone   ☐ Employee referral

☐ Recruitment mailing   ☐ Other

Referral requests	Date sent	Date received
1. _____	_____	_____
2. _____	_____	_____
3. _____	_____	_____
Application	_____	_____
Contract	_____	_____
Pre-camp materials	_____	_____

Interview date _____

Comments _____

_____

Telephone contacts and referrals _____

_____

Subject _____

Selected for position _____

Rejected for position _____

Reason for rejection _____

_____

Staff Interview Notes

This is an example of a form that the employer might use to guide questions and keep notes during an interview.

Name _____

Address (school)_____

_____

Address (permanent)_____

_____

Age (by June 1) _____

Educational level _____

Major _____

Staff positions _____

Previous camp experience _____

_____

Other pertinent experiences_____

_____

Certifications_____

References known to camp_____

_____

Other observations_____

_____

Staff Interview Questions

This is an example of questions the employer might use to interview prospective staff.

1. Tell me about your previous camp experiences.
2. Tell me about your most memorable camp experience — your best time; your worst time.
3. Tell me about your college or university experiences and your extracurricular activities.
4. What are some of your strongest leadership skills?
5. What have you learned about yourself in the last year from your experiences at college (in high school)?
6. How would your supervisor from your last job describe you?
7. Tell me about your ability to work with others.
8. Why do you want to work for us?
9. Tell me about your strengths in working with children and on what experience you base your conclusions.
10. What qualities do you most admire in yourself?
11. What are some areas in which you believe you can improve?
12. In what areas do you feel you will need the most support?
13. Are there any reasons why I shouldn't hire you?

Checklist

It is important that you understand the following:
Potential staff members should understand that campers' needs for health, safety and happiness comes first. Fun and learning is important in relationship to the care given to the campers.
Illegal drugs and alcohol are strictly forbidden. Abuse of this policy is *grounds for immediate dismissal.*
Coed visitation in restricted areas is grounds for dismissal.
Appropriate dress is important. Neatness and cleanliness give campers good examples.
You are expected to abide by all policies and procedures with a positive attitude.

(Adapted from Camp Barney Medintz, Cleveland, Ga.)

Staff Interview Form

Position offered _____

Salary offered _____ Date _____

Name _____

Salary requested _____

Permanent address _____

School _____

Birthdate _____

Education completed _____

☐ Poor ☐ Average ☐ Excellent   Appearance (neatness, manners, habits) _____

_____

☐ Poor ☐ Average ☐ Excellent   Communication skills (verbal expression, organization) _____

_____

☐ Poor ☐ Average ☐ Excellent   Maturity (responsiveness, aspirations) _____

_____

☐ Poor ☐ Average ☐ Excellent   Leadership (participation in activities, offices held) _____

_____

☐ Poor ☐ Average ☐ Excellent   Ability to relate to others (sense of humor, warmth, patience)

_____

☐ Poor ☐ Average ☐ Excellent   Overall evaluation _____

_____

☐ Poor ☐ Average ☐ Excellent   Accomplishments and work experience _____

_____

☐ Poor ☐ Average ☐ Excellent   Interpersonal skills _____

Goals and interests related to camp _____

_____

This applicant should be hired: ☐ Yes ☐ No ☐ Reservations

If the answer is other than yes, state why _____

_____

This applicant will need supervision in _____

_____

This applicant will work well with age group _____

This applicant will work well with activity area_____

_____

Thoughts on Being a Camp Counselor

This form is an example of information that might be mailed to a counselor before pre-camp staff training.

Being a camp counselor is one of the most enjoyable positions available to a young person but it is also hard work. It involves dealing with children and your peers on a continuous basis. It calls for both physical and emotional stamina and is very demanding. On the other hand, it is a very rewarding job, and gives you outstanding experiences with others and a chance to sharpen your human relations and physical skills. A camp experience also allows you to see yourself among other adults, to be evaluated on almost a continuous basis on the tasks you are assigned, and to experiment with leadership styles.

1. The group counselor is the liaison between camp administration and the campers. If the counselor does not perform his/her job adequately, no amount of programming, philosophy, or objective setting will achieve a satisfactory summer for the campers (or for that matter, the counselor).
2. The counselor must strive for an ideal that can be respected by the campers. Respect is a quality earned by the counselor and cannot be demanded or ordered.
3. The counselor is not the camper's parent nor his/her teacher but rather presents an image that campers respect and desire to emulate as he/she reaches the counselor's age. This means the staff member leaves an indelible mark on the camper, which the camper will ideally tend to imitate.
4. The counselor must be totally committed on an emotional and intellectual level to the objectives of the camp and the children in his/her care.
5. The counselor must have decided prior to accepting a position at camp that this experience can be extraordinarily important in the life and growth process of each camper.
6. In the short period of a camp season, the counselor has the ability to strengthen the confidence of a child. A poor approach can cause the child to have an unpleasant summer. A positive approach may help the child along the way to a strong self-image.

7. The counselor should be aware campers in his/her care come from varied environments and structures within our society. They come to camp with all the assets and liabilities of each background. Cultivation of the talent and behavior necessary to fulfill their adult roles becomes a significant aspect of the camp environment for the counselor.

8. The sensitive counselor is aware that each child in his/her group possesses latent interests and talents, the development of which could substantially enrich camp life for that camper and perhaps, the group and entire camp. In this regard, it is important for the counselor to express and encourage individuality and creativity.

 ## Important Factors to Remember About Seasonal Staff

1. Often, counselors are students who just finished studying for final examinations. They may have little time to go from student to responsible staff member, and this will have an affect on the job they do.

2. Many staff are worried about finding summer jobs related to their field.

3. College students are accustomed to being on their own; therefore, restrictions of camp life may be difficult. Transition from apartment living to camp living is a big change for a young person who might have just experienced their first taste of freedom from family restraints.

4. Reasons vary for working in camp — altruism, skill building, etc.

5. As college costs rise, so must camp salaries.

6. Counselors will probably challenge camp rules, regulations and philosophies.

7. Written references are difficult to obtain.

8. Be honest. Paint a realistic picture for new staff.

Objectives of Staff Training

These are examples of the objectives you might set for staff training.

You will need to establish objectives before you determine the content of staff training. Once objectives have been set, the steps to successfully complete these objectives should lead to setting the schedule, covering various subjects, completing tasks that will provide a satisfactory experience for staff. Objectives might include:

1. To provide an opportunity for staff to get acquainted with each other and to develop a working relationship.
2. To allow time for staff to become familiar with the program resources of the site and facility.
3. To provide opportunity for the staff to understand and help establish personal, program, and overall camp objectives.
4. To help staff understand how to implement the camp's objectives through program activities.
5. To provide an opportunity for staff to follow the routines of a camp day.
6. To give staff the opportunity to improve and to practice skills necessary to program effectively at camp.
7. To integrate new and former staff into a cohesive group.
8. To demonstrate and use the procedures necessary to effectively function at camp.
9. To develop programming ideas for special events, evening and daily activities.
10. To help staff become familiar with the characteristics of the camper group to be served.
11. To help staff become familiar with assigned campers through discussions, and review of camp records and parent-completed forms.
12. To help staff become familiar with the camp's philosophy on behavior management.
13. To help staff learn about camp's health and safety procedures in camp and to practice these procedures.

General Topic Outline

The following topics for discussion, seminars, workshops, and working sessions should be included in any pre-camp training program for staff.

Administrative Areas

1. Background, history, development of the camp
2. Philosophy and objectives of the organization
3. Staff relationships and organization chart
4. Personnel policies — review of staff manuals, rules and regulations
5. Records and reports that must be filled out
6. Routines — arrival and departure of campers, meal time, rest hour, mail, etc.
7. Maintenance of site and facilities

Counseling and Skill Areas

1. Responsibilities of a camp staff-group and program
2. Equipment and facilities
3. Guidance of campers and characteristics of children
4. Skills — review and training (OLS, waterfront, crafts, music, etc.)
5. Game sessions
6. Group dynamics

Programming Areas

1. How it functions, assigned activities, free choice, etc.
2. Staff responsibilities regarding program activities
3. Ordering program materials
4. Special programs — overnight trip, visitors on site, field days, trips, themes
5. Religious or spiritual life at camp

Techniques

1. Role-playing — group and multiple
2. Group discussion
3. Actual skill lessons
4. Films
5. Tape recordings
6. Consultants

Training Opportunities

- American Red Cross courses
- First aid and CPR
- Various types of aquatic training and certification
- ACA Outdoor Living Skills courses
- Courses on child abuse, health problems, wheelchair mobility, etc.
- Activity training (i.e., archery, riflery, backpacking, outdoor living skills, canoeing, rowing, etc.) taught at colleges and universities, or at spring workshops sponsored by ACA Sections or related associations

Specific Topic Planning Form

This is an example of a form that might be used for organizing time frames and speakers for staff training, once you have decided what topics are to be covered.

Beside each topic, list the name of the person who will discuss the topic and make notes on what information they should include.

Administrative Topics	*Time Allotted*	*Trainer*
● Laundry	_____	_____
● Mail, in and out	_____	_____
● Phone calls, in and out	_____	_____
● Money/valuables, campers/staff	_____	_____
● Main office procedures	_____	_____
● Boys/girls campus	_____	_____
● Program office	_____	_____
● Maintenance	_____	_____
● Shower house	_____	_____
● Cabin	_____	_____
● Activity areas	_____	_____
● Light bulbs, etc.	_____	_____
● Pay advances	_____	_____
● Personal vehicles	_____	_____
● Camp vehicles	_____	_____
● Day off transportation	_____	_____
● ACA standards	_____	_____

Staff-Only Topics	*Time Allotted*	*Trainer*
● Time off	_____	_____
● On-duty system	_____	_____
● Staff curfew	_____	_____
● After "taps"	_____	_____
● Activity/general staff	_____	_____
● Appropriate dress	_____	_____
● Staff evaluations	_____	_____
● Staff lounge	_____	_____
● Staff recreation	_____	_____
● Staff visitors	_____	_____

Program Topics	*Time Allotted*	*Trainer*
● Daily	_____	_____
● Special	_____	_____
● Evening	_____	_____
● Coed	_____	_____

	Time Allotted	Trainer
● Movies	_____	_____
● Bedtime	_____	_____
● Cabin signs	_____	_____
● Bunk/division projects	_____	_____
● Rainy-day program/behavior	_____	_____
● Meals/dining room behavior	_____	_____
● Line up	_____	_____
● Announcements	_____	_____

Camper Topics	*Time Allotted*	*Trainer*
● Characteristics	_____	_____
● Behavior	_____	_____
● Recordkeeping	_____	_____
● Homesickness	_____	_____
● Dress	_____	_____
● Assignments	_____	_____

Health Topics	*Time Allotted*	*Trainer*
● General safety	_____	_____
● Clean-up	_____	_____
● Food in bunks	_____	_____
● Cabin clean-up	_____	_____
● Medical records	_____	_____
● Health center procedures	_____	_____
● Drugs — prescription and nonprescription	_____	_____
● Showers	_____	_____

First-Day Procedure Topics	*Time Allotted*	*Trainer*
● Welcome — bus/car arrivals	_____	_____
● Parents in cabin	_____	_____
● Unpacking	_____	_____
● Swimming	_____	_____
● Post cards to home	_____	_____
● Evening home	_____	_____

Other Topics	*Time Allotted*	*Trainer*
● Child abuse	_____	_____
● General demeanor	_____	_____
● Gossip/rumors	_____	_____
● Library	_____	_____
● Parental wishes	_____	_____
● Parental concerns	_____	_____
● Supplies/equipment	_____	_____
● General questions	_____	_____
● Miscellaneous	_____	_____

Personnel Practices and Policies

This list presents examples of policies and practices that should be covered with staff.

Definition of Terms

- **Policy** — declaration of intent and a plan of action (to achieve camp goals). A policy is one of the general guidelines of management.
- **Practice** — established custom or accepted way of doing things.
- **Procedure** — method for implementing a policy.
- **Rule** — authoritative direction for the control of action.

Personnel policies, rules and regulations are generally established and adopted for the mutual protection and benefit of the individual and the agency.

General Comments

1. Personnel policies and practices should be clearly written and succinct.
2. Personnel policies and practices should be provided to and considered by the potential staff member before signing a contract.
3. The camp board (or committee) should be aware of, and in agreement with, established personnel policies and practices or employment agreement.
4. The personnel policies and practices should apply equally and fairly to each employee.
5. Personnel policies and practices should be reviewed annually.
6. The staff should have the opportunity to review personnel policies and practices and to recommend changes to the camp director and/or camp board.

Contractual agreements often include personnel policies and practices. These may include the following topics. Consult the *ACA Standards for Day and Resident Camps,* for additional information.

1. Salary/Remuneration
   a. disbursement
   b. transportation
   c. room and board
   d. tips and gratuities
   e. extras (i.e., camp shirts, etc.)

2. Termination of agreement
    a. dismissals
    b. resignations
3. Sick and emergency leave
    a. absence from work
4. Health
    a. examination and history
    b. hospitalization
    c. insurance
5. Personal behavior
    a. drugs
    b. alcohol
    c. dress
    d. sexual behavior
    e. other
6. Time off
    a. daily
    b. days and evenings off
7. Automobiles
    a. use of private vehicles
    b. use of camp vehicles
    c. parking areas
    d. insurance
8. Telephone calls and telephone use
    a. incoming and outgoing calls for staff
9. Individual and group photographs
10. Pets
11. College credit
12. Firearms
13. Personal belongings and insurance
14. Miscellaneous

Staff Manuals

1. Organizational chart with names/positions of all persons at camp
2. History and philosophy of the camp including information about the agency/founders
3. Goals and objectives — general and specific
4. Personnel policies and camp rules as they effect all staff members — counseling, program, and administrative
5. Suggestions for days off, visitors, etc.
6. Map of the camp site
7. Employment conditions, sick leave, emergency leave, etc.
8. In-service training opportunities
9. Evaluation procedures
10. Camp program schedules including routines such as mail, laundry, daily events, special days, and special events
11. Emergency procedures — fire-prevention information, fire drills, lightening storms, tornadoes, etc.
12. Forms of all types — requisitions, camper and staff evaluations, child abuse report forms
13. Bibliography of books, games, etc., available at camp
14. First aid information
15. Policies as they pertain to the health-care center procedures, transporting campers, tripping, etc.
16. Opening- and closing-day procedures
17. Information pertaining to campers' ages, health, and religious backgrounds, and other pertinent camper information
18. Games, songs, counseling books, and other resources

Pros and Cons of Mailing Staff Training Manuals Prior to In-Camp Training

Pros

- Providing the manual prior to the camp season heightens the staffs' excitement level. It also gives staff an opportunity to learn about the camp and their role at camp.
- It allows you more effective use of time during training sessions.
- It indicates to the staff that you are organized and that forethought has gone into training.

● It gives some indication of what to expect during staff training.

Cons

● The manual usually gets lost and you must replace it.
● Staff members may forget to bring the manual with them to camp.
● Staff often do not read the manual because as students they are getting ready for school exams or taking vacations before coming to camp.
● So many ideas in writing may stifle or overwhelm new staff members.

Staff Evaluation of Camp Season

Please comment on the following in a constructive manner as a way to help us improve our program, staff training, etc. We need suggestions so that appropriate changes can be made. Whether you sign the form or not, it will be seriously considered.

1. Staff training — did it help set the stage for the season?

   _____

   Areas that needed more discussion? Changes? _____

   _____

2. Staff days off, time off, staff policies, staff evening programs, assignments, etc._____

   _____

3. Programming — activity schedules, choices, continuity

   _____

4. Facilities — need and changes _____

   _____

5. Health care center _____

6. Dining room and service _____

7. Canteen and mail _____

8. Miscellaneous _____

What the Heck Is a CIT?

Counselor-In-Training programs should be geared to training young people for a staff role in a day or resident camp. Each CIT should become familiar with the roles played by a counselor in the day-to-day living situation at camp. If the aims and objectives of the program are to be met, it is important to use as many learning situations as possible with the young people involved. CITs who assume responsibility for the day-to-day care of their own area and the governance and behavior of their CIT group are practicing skills necessary for successful leadership.

Who Are They?

CITs may be entering their junior or senior year in high school and they are the type of young people you would want as staff in the future. They may currently be campers who you see as having the potential to be leaders.

What Do You Do With Them?

- Teach them activity skills
- Involve them in camp seminars
- Involve them in camp work programs
- Involve them in camp service programs
- Involve them in their own group activities
- Involve them with campers in skills and in cabin (or group) activities

How Do They Live in a Resident Camp?

- With each other in a designated area
- In cabins with campers, spread throughout the camper age groupings

How Can They Function in a Day Camp?

- With each other in a designated group
- With campers, assigned to a group or activity

What Programs Might They Have?

- Overnights and backpacking trips
- Trips to visit camps
- In and out-of-camp community projects
- Resident camp — days off away from or in camp
- An evening out — dinner and a movie; a cultural event

What Responsibilities Might They Have?

- Their cabin (group) and areas
- Their behavior
- The group's behavior (on a rotating basis)
- Evening or special programs for the entire camp, a unit program, or for their own program

How Do You Find CITs

The easiest way to find CITs is to use the resources you may already have in place.

- Camp brochures and applications
- Word-of-mouth
- Former campers
- Staff recommendations
- Reunions, general recruitment methods (same as for camper recruitment)
- On-going programs — YMCA, YWCA, Girl Scouts of America, church, etc.
- Board, committee, staff members' children
- Campers who are not old enough to be staff members but do not want to be campers again

Goals and Objectives

The following are examples of goals for a Counselor-in-training program.

Goal

To select persons who will be successful in a CIT program.

Objectives

- Develop an application form that provides basic information for the selection of CITs.
- Develop criteria for selection of CITs prior to providing application forms.
- Develop materials that will give prospective CITs and their parents information about the program.

Goal

To train high school students in camping skills.

Objectives

- Set up a training program that will allow high school students activity skills to share with campers and staff.
- Set up a program that will ensure an understanding of the camp environment for those participating in the CIT program.

Goal

To have those trained as CITs return to camp as staff members.

Objectives

- Evaluate the CIT participants in order to recommend those who should be on staff in the future.
- Select those CIT participants who have physical and human-relations skills to work as staff.

Application Questions

This is an example of the kinds of questions a CIT application might include.

Name and address
Birthdate
Parents' names
Brothers/sisters (name and ages)
Business phone for parents
(other personal information camp deems necessary)
High school
Grade in September
Graduation year
Extra-curricular activities
Other organizational affiliations
Offices held in any of the above
Training in first aid, water activities, outdoor living skills, crafts, music, etc.
Hobbies
Camp experience
Camp address (city, state, zip)
Dates
Work experience and position
Employer name and address
Employment dates
References
Paragraph about yourself and why you want to become part of our Counselor-in-Training program
Statement of compliance with CIT program rules
Signature of applicant
Parent's signature acknowledging child's involvement in program
Date

CIT Information Sheet

This is an example of the kinds of additional information you might desire from a CIT after accepting him/her but before camp.

You have been accepted for the CIT program during the summer of 199___.

Please answer the following questions.

1. What would you like to learn and to achieve this summer?

2. What are your goals for the campers you will be working with?

3. What do you think the campers' goals will be?

4. What do you think the goals of the camper's parents are?

5. Are the goals you listed above attainable? Give an example of how you would go about fulfilling the goals you believe can be reached. Also, explain why you think some goals cannot be reached.

CIT Training Topics

This is a list of suggested topics to cover with CITs during training. This form might be used for planning CIT training.

- Goals, objectives, philosophy of camp
- Role of staff members at camp — title and relationship to other staff members and to campers, requirements for positions on the staff
- Personnel policies, staff behavior
- Procedures — dining room, laundry, snacks, mail, infirmary, emergency, etc.
- Program — how it functions and why; skills required in each area; daily and division (unit) programs; special events; rainy day, visitor's day, first- and last-day program, etc.
- ACA camp standards
- Skill specialization — should a CIT specialize?

Seminar/Skill Sessions

- Camper needs
- Camper expectations
- Camper desires
- Parental expectations
- Problem-solving
- Camper behaviors — homesickness, the bully, shy children, bedwetting, unhappy children, etc.
- Age, health considerations, religious, ethnic backgrounds of campers
- Age-group characteristics
- Supervision of campers
- Health, safety needs

Health and Safety Concepts

- Personal health
- Substance abuse
- Child abuse — sexual, physical, emotional
- Child abuse — reporting responsibility
- Accident prevention — risk management
- Camper health needs — allergies, infectious disease control, etc.
- Human sexuality
- First aid, CPR

Emergency Procedures and Crisis Management

- Fire
- Lost camper
- Waterfront
- Accident
- Natural disaster

Conduct Expectations

- CIT conduct
- Camper conduct
- Staff conduct

Other Skills

- Outdoor Living Skills Program
- Waterfront certifications
- Archery
- Riflery
- Song-leading
- Rainy day activities
- Activities related to your camp program

Program Knowledge

- Regular schedule
- Rainy-day schedule
- Weekend schedule
- Special events
- Session change-over
- Opening and closing day
- Visitors' day
- Flexibility
- Traditions

Team Building Skills

- Challenge course
- Trips out of camp
- Work projects
- Governance

CIT Policies and Rules

This is a list of suggested restrictions and privileges that should be covered with CITs. This form might be used in planning CIT training and other activities.

Behavior Regulations

- CITs follow the "usual" camp rules
- Bedtime (later than campers, earlier than staff)
- May not use the counselor lounge
- No individual day off
- May not receive food packages
- No tobacco, alcohol, drugs
- Personal relationships policy
- May not punish campers
- May not be left alone with a group of children

Privilege Possibilities

- Shirts/uniforms
- May leave cabins after camper taps
- Have a CIT lounge or use staff lounge
- Have staff canteen
- Sit at head of table
- May be paid
- Group day off
- May leave camp with a staff member (with permission)
- Night off
- Group trips
- Special foods on a cookout
- Consultants often used for training purposes

Self-Directed Activities

- Group agreement on self-directed governance within limits.
- Code of conduct, rules and regulations should be written with, not for, the group. Group should know limits.
- Identification necessary (i.e., shirts, hats, "graduation," role of the CIT defined for all).

CIT Evaluation

This is an example of questions that could be used by staff for evaluating CITs.

1. Does the CIT have a neat appearance?
2. Is the CIT tactful (speaks truthfully but doesn't unnecessarily offend, or hurt others)?
3. Does the CIT have a friendly personality that attracts others?
4. Is the CIT cooperative (even when carrying out the plans of others)?
5. Can the CIT take as well as give directions?
6. Is the CIT prompt for all camp activities?
7. Does the CIT show initiative (ability to start without outside prodding or suggestions)?
8. Do you feel the CIT can accept criticism and learn from it?
9. Does the CIT refrain from emotional outbursts?
10. Can the CIT objectively make decisions regarding others?
11. Does the CIT have the stamina to last through a strenuous day?
12. Does the CIT exhibit a sense of humor?
13. Does the CIT exhibit a sincere desire to work with children? In an activity?
14. Is the CIT willing to accept responsibility. Is he/she able to fulfill the responsibility? Give examples.
15. Is the CIT able to work well with campers? Give examples.
16. Does the CIT relate well to the counselors? Give examples.
17. How does the CIT contribute to the cabin? Give examples.
18. Does the CIT present a problem to the cabin staff in any way? If so, please explain.
19. Please discuss improvement or lack thereof.
20. Did you, as a counselor, meet with the CIT to help him/her evaluate his/her experiences?
21. Did you feel the CIT was able to understand the campers or camper-group through these meetings.

Index

S

T

U

W